DISCARDED

Here's all the great literature in this grade level of *Celebrate Reading!*

The Deciding Factor
Learning What Matters

Featured Poet
Gary Soto

yum.

Book A Celebrate Reading!

A Volcano of Cheers

Chasing Your Goals

Book B Celebrate Reading!

Featured Poets
Nikki Giovanni
X. J. Kennedy

The First Magnificent Web

Tales of the Imagination

Featured Poets
Jack Prelutsky
Lewis Carroll
Richard Armour
Eve Merriam

Book C Celebrate Reading!

A Better Time Slot
From There to Here

Book D Celebrate Reading!

Trade Books Celebrate Reading!

More Great Books to Read!

The Grizzly
by Annabel and
Edgar Johnson

**Where the Lillies
Bloom**
by Vera and Bill Cleaver

The Master Puppeteer
by Katherine Paterson

**The Bread Sister of
Sinking Creek**
by Robin Moore

Maniac Magee
by Jerry Spinelli

Sweetwater
by Laurence Yep

It's Like This, Cat
by Emily Neville

Let the Hurricane Roar
by Rose Wilder Lane

CHASING YOUR GOALS

A VOLCANO OF CHEERS

TITLES IN THIS SET

The Deciding Factor
A Volcano of Cheers
The First Magnificent Web
A Better Time Slot

Cover Artists
Steve Ewert has been interested in graphic images since he was in high school, but it wasn't until his fourth year of engineering school that he realized he wanted to make photography his medium of expression and his career.

Naomi Spellman credits her painting background for the "painterly effects" she likes to add to the work she does on a computer. She used a color scanner and additional photographs to create a special look for the group photograph taken by Mr. Ewert.

Renée Flower, who did the lettering for *A Volcano of Cheers,* says she first became an artist at four or five when she used baby cream and powder to paint her sister's crib. Today her large paintings usually include words relating to the subject.

ISBN: 0-673-80072-5

Acknowledgments appear on page 144.

5678910RRS9998979695

CHASING YOUR GOALS

A VOLCANO OF CHEERS

ScottForesman

A Division of HarperCollins*Publishers*

CONTENTS

Jerry Spinelli

Maniac Magee

from Maniac Magee

They say Maniac Magee was born in a dump. They say his stomach was a cereal box and his heart a sofa spring.

They say he kept an eight-inch cockroach on a leash and that rats stood guard over him while he slept. They say if you knew he was coming and you sprinkled salt on the ground and he ran over it, within two or three blocks he would be as slow as everybody else.

They say.

What's true, what's myth? It's hard to know.

Finsterwald's gone now, yet even today you'll never find a kid sitting on the steps where he once lived. The Little League field is still there, and the band shell. Cobble's Corner still stands at the corner of Hector and Birch, and if you ask the man behind the counter, he'll take the clump of string out of a drawer and let you see it.

Grade school girls in Two Mills still jump rope and chant:

> Ma-*niac*, Ma-*niac*
> *He's so* cool
> Ma-*niac*, Ma-*niac*
> *Don't go to* school
> *Runs all* night
> *Runs all* right
> Ma-*niac*, Ma-*niac*
> *Kissed a* bull!

And sometimes the girl holding one end of the rope is from the West side of Hector, and the girl on the other is from the East side; and if you're looking for Maniac Magee's legacy, or monument, that's as good as any—even if it wasn't really a bull.

But that's okay, because the history of a kid is one part fact, two parts legend, and three parts snowball. And if you want to know what it was like back when Maniac Magee roamed these parts, well, just run your hand under your movie seat and be very, very careful not to let the facts get mixed up with the truth.

If the Wonders of the World hadn't stopped at seven, Cobble's Knot would have been number eight.

Nobody knew how it got there. As the story goes, the original Mr. Cobble wasn't doing too well with the original Cobble's Corner Grocery at the corner of Hector and Birch. In his first two weeks, all he sold was some Quaker Oats and penny candy.

Then one morning, as he unlocked the front door for business, he saw the Knot. It was dangling from the flagpole that hung over the big picture window, the one that said FROSTED FOODS in icy blue-and-white letters. He got out a pair of scissors and was about to snip it off, when he noticed what an unusual and incredible knot it was.

And then he got an idea. He could offer a prize to anyone who untangled the Knot. Publicize it. Call the newspaper. Winner's picture on the front page, Cobble's Corner in the background. Business would boom.

Well, he went ahead and did it, and if business didn't exactly boom, it must have at least peeped a little, because eons later, when Maniac Magee came to town, Cobble's Corner was still there. Only now it sold pizza instead of groceries. And the prize was different. It had started out being sixty seconds alone with the candy counter; now it was one large pizza per week for a whole year.

Which, in time, made the Knot practically priceless. Which is why, after leaving it outside for a year, Mr. Cobble took it down and kept it in a secret place inside the store and brought it out only to meet a challenger.

If you look at old pictures in the *Two Mills Times*, you see that the Knot was about the size and shape of a lopsided volleyball. It was made of string, but it had more contortions, ins and outs, twists and turns and dips and doodles than the brain of Albert Einstein himself. It had defeated all comers for years, including J. J. Thorndike, who grew up to be a magician, and Fingers Halloway, who grew up to be a pickpocket.

Hardly a week went by without somebody taking a shot at the Knot, and losing. And each loser added to the glory that awaited someone who could untie it.

"So you see," said Amanda,* "if you go up there and untie Cobble's Knot—which I *know* you can—you'll get your picture in the paper and you'll be the biggest hero ever around here and *nooo*-body'll mess with you then."

Maniac listened and thought about it and finally gave a little grin. "Maybe you're just after the pizza, since you know I can't eat it."

Amanda screeched. "Jeff-*freee!*** The pizza's not the point." She started to hit him. He laughed and

*Amanda Beale is Maniac Magee's good friend.
**Maniac's real name is Jeffrey Lionel Magee. He can't eat pizza because it makes him break out in red blotches.

grabbed her wrists. And he said okay, he'd give it a try.

They brought out the Knot and hung it from the flagpole. They brought out the official square wooden table for the challenger to stand on, and from the moment Maniac climbed up, you could tell the Knot was in big trouble.

To the ordinary person, Cobble's Knot was about as friendly as a nest of yellowjackets. Besides the tangle itself, there was the weathering of that first year, when the Knot hung outside and became hard as a rock. You could barely make out the individual strands. It was grimy, moldy, crusted over. Here and there a loop stuck out, maybe big enough to stick your pinky finger through, pitiful testimony to the challengers who had tried and failed.

And there stood Maniac, turning the Knot, checking it out. Some say there was a faint grin on his face, kind of playful, as though the Knot wasn't his enemy at all, but an old pal just playing a little trick on him. Others say his mouth was more grim than grin, that his eyes lit up like flashbulbs, because he knew he was finally facing a knot that would stand up and fight, a worthy opponent.

He lifted it in his hands to feel the weight of it. He touched it here and touched it there, gently, daintily. He scraped a patch of crust off with his fingernail. He laid his fingertips on it, as though feeling for a pulse.

Only a few people were watching at first, and half of them were Heck's Angels, a roving tricycle gang of four- and five-year-olds. Most of them had had sneaker-lace or yo-yo knots untied by Maniac, and they expected this would only take a couple of seconds longer. When the seconds became minutes, they started to get antsy, and before ten minutes had passed, they were zooming off in search of somebody to terrorize.

The rest of the spectators watched Maniac poke and tug and pick at the knot. Never a big pull or yank, just his fingertips touching and grazing and peck-pecking away, like some little bird.

"What's he doin'?" somebody said.

"What's taking so long?"

"He gonna do it or not?"

After an hour, except for a few more finger-size loops, all Maniac had to show for his trouble were the flakes of knot crust that covered the table.

"He ain't even found the end of the string yet," somebody grumbled, and almost everybody but Amanda took off.

Maniac never noticed. He just went on working.

By lunchtime they were all back, and more kept coming. Not only kids, but grownups, too, black and white, because Cobble's Corner was on Hector, and word was racing through the neighborhoods on both the east and west sides of the street.

What people saw they didn't believe.

The knot had grown, swelled, exploded. It was a frizzy globe—the newspaper the next day described it as a "gigantic hairball." Now, except for a packed-in clump at the center, it was practically all loops. You could look through it and see Maniac calmly working on the other side.

"He found the end!" somebody gasped, and the corner burst into applause.

Meanwhile, inside, Cobble's was selling pizza left

and right, not to mention zeps (a Two Mills type of hoagie), steak sandwiches, strombolis, and gallons of soda. Mr. Cobble himself came out to offer Maniac some pizza, which Maniac of course politely turned down. He did accept an orange soda, though, and then a little kid, whose sneaker laces Maniac had untied many a time, handed up to him a three-pack of Tastykake butterscotch Krimpets.

After polishing off the Krimpets, Maniac did the last thing anybody expected: he lay down and took a nap right there on the table, the knot hanging above him like a small hairy planet, the mob buzzing all around him. Maniac knew what the rest of them didn't: the hardest part was yet to come. He had to find the right routes to untangle the mess, or it would just close up again like a rock and probably stay that way forever. He would need the touch of a surgeon, the alertness of an owl, the cunning of three foxes, and the foresight of a grand master in chess. To accomplish that, he needed to clear his head, to flush away all distraction, especially the memory of the butterscotch Krimpets, which had already hooked him.

In exactly fifteen minutes, he woke up and started back in.

Like some fairytale tailor, he threaded the end through the maze, dipping and doodling through openings the way he squiggled a football through a defense. As the long August afternoon boiled along, the exploded knot-hairball would cave in here, cave in there. It got lumpy, out of shape, saggy. The *Times* photographer made starbursts with his camera. The people munched on Cobble's pizza and spilled across Hector from sidewalk to sidewalk and said "Ouuuu!" and "Ahhhh!"

And then, around dinnertime, a huge roar went up, a volcano of cheers. Cobble's Knot was dead. Undone. Gone. It was nothing but string.

Bugles, cap guns, sirens, firecrackers, war whoops . . . Cobble's Corner was a madhouse.

Traffic had to beep and inch through the mob. Kids cried for autographs. Scraps of paper fluttered down in a shower of homemade confetti.

A beaming Mr. Cobble handed up a certificate to Maniac for the year's worth of large pizzas. Maniac accepted it and said his thanks. The undone knot lay in a coiled heap at Maniac's feet. Mr. Cobble grabbed it. Already people were guessing how long it was.*

---

*It turned out to be four and a half blocks long. Someone tied it to a stop sign and started walking, and that's how far he got before it gave out.

B·16

Where Maniac Came From

Jerry Spinelli

There are many sources for *Maniac Magee*, since the novel, like most works, is a patchwork quilt with many pieces of different origins.

Maniac himself was based on a friend of mine, who was a foundling dropped off on the doorstep of a judge and who grew up in an orphanage. Since he had no bike or skateboard, his main method of transportation was running—three miles to the hoagie shop, six miles to the movies. The idea of his constant running and the simplicity of his mode of transportation appealed to me, and I filed away this seed until the time was ripe for a story.

When I came to write *Maniac Magee*, the running became a metaphor. Maniac was free, uncomplicated, and pure. As his means of travel is pure, so are his dealings with the rest of the world. Maniac is colorblind; he doesn't see the racial distinctions that we are taught to see. He is not socialized.

Like my friend who grew up in the orphanage, Maniac has vague origins. In this way, Maniac becomes mythic, a legend. He is a throwback to more innocent times. As I say in the book's introduction, "The history of a kid is one part fact, two parts legend, and three parts snowball."

Another source for *Maniac* was a coach I had in Knee-Hi baseball (a step up from Little League) when I was about thirteen. The coach pitched a stopball that nobody could hit —a ball he claimed stopped when it reached the plate, waited for the batter to swing, and then continued into the catcher's mitt. The pitch was really a sloppy, slow knuckleball, but few kids ever laid good wood on it. I describe this pitch later on in the novel in conjunction with a character named Grayson.

1. Maniac Magee impresses people when he untangles the knot. Think of someone who has impressed you. Why were you impressed? Is this person at all like Maniac Magee?

2. The author says "The history of a kid is one part fact, two parts legend, and three parts snowball." What's fact, what's legend, and what's snowball in the story of Maniac Magee?

3. Brainstorm ideas and list at least three problems that might challenge Maniac Magee.

Another Book About a Winner
In *Red-Hot Hightops* by Matt Christopher, Kelly finds that a mysterious pair of red hightop sneakers makes her a better basketball player.

basketball

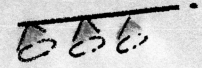

when spanky goes
to the playground all the big boys say
   hey big time—what's happenin'
'cause his big brother plays basketball
   for their high school
and he gives them the power sign and says
   you got it
but when i go and say
   what's the word
they just say
   your nose is running junior

one day i'll be seven feet tall
even if i never get a big brother
and i'll stuff that sweaty ball down
their laughing throats

Nikki Giovanni

Basketball Bragging

Agatha Goop with a whale of a whoop
Swept a swisher through the hoop.

She told her teammates, "There you are!
You guys are dog meat! I'm the star!"

Her teammates knew just what to do:
They dribbled her down and dunked her through.

Now Agatha's nose may be out of joint,
But she had to admit that they'd made their point.

X. J. Kennedy

Billie Wind Listens to Her Land

illie Wind could see the orange tree through the open walls of the council house. A white bird floated down upon it, and she wondered if it had a nest nearby.

"Billie Wind." The medicine man was speaking. "May I have your attention?" She was standing beside her sister Mary in the dim light of the house. Outside the sunlight was white and hot. Inside a soft trade wind blew under the palm-thatched roof, cooling the air pleasantly. Charlie Wind, the medicine man, who was also her uncle and friend, cleared his throat.

"Billie Wind Listens to Her Land" is from pp. *1–31 in* The Talking Earth *by Jean Craighead George. Copyright © 1983 by Jean Craighead George. Reprinted by permission of HarperCollins Publishers.*

B·23

"Billie Wind," he repeated. "May I have your attention?" She promptly looked from the bird to the dark eyes of the elderly man.

"It is told that you do not believe in the animal gods who talk." He frowned.

"It is told that you do not believe that there is a great serpent who lives in the Everglades and punishes bad Seminoles." He shook his head, then cast a sober glance at the councilmen, who were seated on the hard earth around him.

"And it is told that you doubt that there are little people who live underground and play tricks on our people." He pulled his white Seminole cape closer around his lean shoulders, forcing Billie Wind to notice that it was too long. It almost touched the black-and-white border of his skirt.

"Are you listening to me?"

"Yes," she answered and smiled, tightening her lips so she would not giggle.

"The council has met. We are disturbed by your doubts."

Billie Wind caught her breath. She knew perfectly well these men did not believe in the serpent and the talking animals and the dwarfs. They were educated and wise men. She knew them well. Several were her uncles, others were the fathers of her best friends. She waited for them to laugh understandingly as they usually did when the old legends and beliefs were discussed.

But they did not even smile. Charlie Wind crossed his arms on his chest.

"We are a tribe of the Seminole Indians," he said in a solemn voice. "We believe that each person is part of the Great Spirit who is the wind and the rain and the sun and the earth, and the air above the earth. Therefore we can not order or command anyone." He paused. "But we do agree that you should be punished for being a doubter."

Billie Wind glanced from face to face, searching for the good humor that would soon end this to-do about serpents and dwarfs. No one smiled, not even her comical uncle, Three-Hands-on-the-Saddle.

"What do you think would be a suitable punishment for you, Billie Wind?"

She let her mind wander, waiting for someone to break the silence and send her off to play. When it became apparent that this would not happen, she concentrated on a punishment: something ridiculous, something they would not let her do, it would be so dangerous.

"I think," she said with dignity, "that I should go into the pa-hay-okee, the Everglades, where these spirits dwell, and stay until I hear the animals talk, see the serpent and meet the little people who live underground."

She waited for Charlie Wind to shake his head "no."

"Good," he said, much to her surprise. Promptly he turned to Mary Wind, who was two years older than she.

"Mary Wind," he said to the sturdy fifteen-year-old, who had been the one to tell the medicine man about Billie Wind's doubts, "go with your sister in the tribal dugout as far as Lost Dog Island. There you will find an ancient dugout pulled up on the alligator beach. In it are three white heron feathers. Wave them over Billie Wind so that she will have a safe journey. Then come on home."

Crossing his feet, he sat down among the councilmen, who were meeting, as they did once a year, on the tribal island of Panther Paw in the Everglades to settle arguments and reprimand the offenders of the Seminole laws. The Big Cypress Reservation, where they farmed and raised cattle, was about thirty miles west of their island. Most of the clan would return to their farms and homes after the four-day Green Corn Dance festival that would start the day after tomorrow.

Billie Wind was well known for her curiosity. Only last summer she had peeked through the cane screen at the rear of the council house to watch Charlie Wind open the sacred medicine bundle. Her foot had slipped, and she had knocked the screen over.

"What are you doing?" he had asked in surprise.

"Trying to see the magic in the medicine bundle," she had answered. "I want to see what makes the rain fall and cures the sick."

"And what did you see?"

"Nothing," she had answered honestly. "Just some minerals and stones, a snake's fang and the flint and steel you start the Green Corn Dance fires with—also some herbs." She had tipped her head inquiringly. "Do they *really* make the rain fall and cure the sick?"

Charlie Wind had not answered immediately. Instead he had reached for a feather broom, swept the ground, sat down and gestured for her to sit beside him.

"The medicine bundle," he had said, leaning so close that she could see the dust in the wrinkles of his face, "was given to two ancient medicine men by the adopted son of the Corn Mother.

"The bundle was divided between them, and they divided their bundles into forty more—one for each clan. When the Spaniards came to Florida they killed and ravaged and warred upon the ancient people. Most of the medicine bundles were burned or lost. Some were hidden and never have been found again. Only eight still exist. And this is one of them." He reverently patted the leather pouch with his long fingers. "And that makes it magical to me."

"But it doesn't really make the rain fall, does it, Charlie Wind?"

"Yes," he had answered.

"But you have asked the sky to rain every day for a year and it hasn't rained. South Florida is still dry. Our gardens are shriveling."

"You are too practical," he said. "That is the white man's trait. There is more to the Earth than only the things you can see with your eyes."

"What are they?" she asked with great sincerity. "I would love to see what isn't there."

"You are a doubter." He shook his head; then, holding his hands, palms up, to the sky, he closed his eyes.

Presently he opened them.

"I will teach you how to see something that is not there," he had said. "You must find two lightning bolts and bring them to me."

"Two lightning bolts?" she said with astonishment. "I can't do that."

"You must. Then you will see. Now, go along and find them." He dismissed her with the back of his hand.

Billie Wind walked out of the council house and leaned against the trunk of an avocado tree. A mourning dove cooed to her large babies, who were balanced on a limb above Billie. Billie Wind studied them as if the answer to this odd assignment would come from the lovely birds. No answer. Perhaps an inspiration would come from her grandmother in the communal kitchen, who was bent over the fire stirring a pot with one hand while holding her full, bright, yellow-and-red skirt with the other. None came. She glanced at her family's chickee, an open home with a platform for sleeping and a roof thatched with palm leaves. Her mother, Whispering Wind, was at the sewing machine, pumping it with her foot and putting together small pieces of bright cotton. She saw no lightning bolts there; just Whispering Wind's warm silhouette against the sunny sky.

She wondered how her mother would solve this problem. Whispering Wind would think of something; for, like Billie, she was very practical. She had to be. She was the head of the Wind Clan and dealt with many problems that the medicine man and the councilmen did not: settling arguments, encouraging leadership and giving self-confidence.

"Lightning bolts," Billie Wind mumbled. "Where? Where?"

On the far side of the open common another uncle was stirring the ceremonial cauldron as he brewed red willow, lizard's-tail plants and ginseng. He sang as he mixed the "black drink," a special brew that is made once a year for the Green Corn Dance. She smiled. The black drink was a lightning bolt if ever there was one. When the councilmen drank it on the second day of the festival they danced like tornadoes and threw spears higher than rockets could soar. They saw demons and future events, then fell as if struck by lightning.

"I'll bring Charlie Wind two cups of the black drink," she said mischievously, then became serious. "Where am I going to find two lightning bolts? Does Charlie Wind want me to say I can not find any? What does he want? Lightning strikes and is gone. It leaps from cloud to cloud, and cloud to ground. It does not stay still. I can not catch it.

"And Charlie Wind knows that. So what does he want of me?"

"Billie Wind," her mother called. "Come to the chickee. You must finish stitching your dancing shoes for the festival." Mamau Whispering Wind was seated cross-legged on the table-high platform in the chickee. Beside her lay pillows, pots, dishes, a radio, canned foods, blankets and a sewing machine. The earthen floor of the chickee had been swept clean for the day.

"I can't right now," Billie Wind said. "I have to perform a miracle for Charlie Wind." She sighed and her mother's eyes softened kindly as if to say: "So he's up to miracles again."

The shoes Billie Wind was making were for the dances that celebrated the ripening of the corn crop the Seminoles grew in their gardens. The festival was only one day away, and she had hours of work before her. She must also make a turban for her brother. This year he had been chosen to go into the pa-hay-okee to kill and bring home a white heron. The feathers would be hung from the poles that would be carried in the Feather Dance. She should not be wasting time looking for lightning bolts that could not be found. She should be getting ready for the day after tomorrow, a hallowed day in late June.

On that day the men and boys would clean the dancing ground, repair chickees and take ceremonial baths. They would gather wood, and Charlie Wind would light the fire after sundown. There would be dancing and games. On the next day the men would feast in the council house, then join the rest of the tribe with more dancing and game playing.

On the third day the medicine man would bathe and bring out the sacred medicine bundle. Charlie Wind would open it before the councilmen and they would pass judgment on those who had disobeyed

the tribal laws. They would then toss the first corn
of the year into the black drink and drink it at mid-
night. The Feather Dance, the Woodpecker Dance
and the Buffalo Dance would be performed until
the sun came up. Billie Wind would dance with the
women. On the dawn of the fourth day the sacred
bundle would be hidden for another year, and
when that was done the entire tribe would feast on
the new corn. They would dance in celebration of
all the forces that had made the harvest a success:
the sun, the rain, the darkness of night and all the
animals that they had seen during the good season.

With all this excitement to prepare for, Billie
Wind was annoyed that she had to find two lightning bolts. She kicked a stone and wondered what
to do. She would turn around in a complete circle,
and if no idea came, she would give up.

Halfway around she saw two spider lilies far out
in the saw grass. Their long white petals folded back
from thin golden centers like the sparks of a lightning bolt. She rolled up her blue jeans, waded out
through the shallow glades to the lilies and with a
flick of her penknife cut off the flowers. Then she
splashed back to Panther Paw Island.

"Here are the lightning bolts," she had said to
Charlie Wind, her eyes shining with the fun of her
joke. She waited for him to send her out for real
lightning bolts. He did not.

"Yes," he said, looking closely at the flowers.
"They are indeed."

Billie Wind stared at the medicine man as if to see
the circuits and cells inside his head that made him
think so strangely.

"Yes," he repeated. "These *are* lightning bolts."
And for a flash of a moment Billie Wind almost
understood something profound; but not quite.

That had been a year ago. And now, here she was again, led into trouble by her curiosity.

"The tribal dugout will be waiting for you at the airboat dock tomorrow morning at sunup," Charlie Wind said. "Stay one night and two days and come home."

She walked out of the council house, wondering why she had imposed such a punishment on herself. She wanted to dance and play games. Why hadn't she suggested she sweep the dancing ground? The councilmen would have accepted that as punishment. But no, she was so stubborn and curious she had to suggest a crazy long voyage. She walked home and sat in the shadow of the chickee, feeling sorry for herself.

The next morning she was cheered by the rising sun. It shone like a red penny through the mist. She woke Mary, and they walked through the silvery dew to the dugout. It was tied beside the airboat, a flat boat with a motorized fan that "blew" passengers across the saw grass in the watery prairie the Indians called the pa-hay-okee. She looked at the airboat, which carried the children to the Indian school on Big Cypress Reservation and the men to islands to hunt and fish. Then she looked at the dugout, a beautiful, simple craft chopped and burned from a cypress tree by Charlie Wind himself.

"Sit in the bow," she said to Mary, who wore her traditional Seminole cape for the occasion, an airy circle of cloth with a hole in the center for her head. It fell gracefully over her shoulders to her waist. Below she wore a skirt of brilliantly colored patchwork, the hallmark of the Seminole Indians. The skirt was made of tiny patches, one inch square and smaller, sewn together to form intricate designs. Mary's was a blue, green, yellow and black mosaic and was startlingly beautiful. Billie Wind looked at her sister.

"Why did you tell Charlie Wind on me?"

"Because you are too scientific. You are realistic like the white men."

"I see what I see. What I don't see, I don't believe."

"You were not that way before you went to the school at the Kennedy Space Center when our father worked for the scientists."

"That's not true. I've always been curious. I want answers, not legends. What is the matter with that?"

"What is the matter with that? I'll tell you. Someday you will be the head of your family and you'll need to know more than facts."

Billie Wind did not answer her. Lost Dog Island was just ahead; she would be glad to be rid of Mary and alone in the glades. The sun was up, the frogs had quieted down and the birds were calling to each other as they awoke and assembled for the day. She could take just so much of her sister and all her righteousness. She poled swiftly.

Billie Wind was tall for her age. Her frame was lithe like a reed, a gift from her Calusa ancestors who had lived in the Everglades for unknown thousands of years before the Spanish conquistadores arrived in the late 1550s. Her high cheekbones were reminiscent of her Hitchiti ancestors, members of the Creek Confederacy who were driven out of Georgia by the Colonial Army around 1750. The Creeks had joined forces with escaped Black slaves and, as one clan, they had crossed Lake Okeechobee and vanished into what the white men called, at that time, the unholy swamp. Here they had lived well on the abundant game, fruits and succulent plants. Isolated in the wilderness they had become proud and independent and had established governments to help them live in balance with the land. They had never signed a peace treaty with the U.S. government. Even today they are at war with the United States. The white men called these strong, intelligent people the Sem-in-oli, meaning "wild" in the Hitchiti language.

Billie Wind was approaching Lost Dog Island on a hundred-year-old alligator trail, a trail swept free of grass and plants by the heavy reptiles dragging tails and bodies from one island or pool to the next. She watched for alligators as she poled. A big one, ten to twelve feet long, could upset a dugout with one whack of its tail. She saw only one small gator. As she approached the island she leaned on her pole and sent the boat flying up onto the beach.

"I see the dugout," Mary said brightly and, checking the beach for alligators, stepped ashore. She quickly found the feathers and turned around just as Billie Wind gave her boat a shove and slid out into the water.

"Billie Wind. Come back!" Mary shouted. "Charlie Wind told me. . . . "

"I don't want any silly feathers waved over my boat," she answered, poling into the deep water at the end of the island.

"Billie Wind." Mary's voice broke into many voices as it bounced off the thousands of three-sided saw grass blades nourished by the shallow waters of the glades. When the sound finally reached Billie's ear it was more like a lost ibis crying than her sister. She rounded the island and poled until she could not hear Mary anymore, then she stopped and looked at the glittering Everglades, the river of grass, the unholy swamp, the pa-hay-okee.

ach saw grass blade glistened like a copper spear in the hot June sun. Many hundreds of white birds skimmed over the swamp water. Their reflections skimmed under them. In the distance, gray-green islands like Panther Paw resembled ships sailing against the brilliant blue sky. The Everglades was flat and as luminous as winter's southern seas.

And that was all she saw—grass-filled water, birds, sky and islands like her own. She was in an immense wilderness larger than the state of Delaware, and as glorious as birds in flight.

She felt comforted. Her hurt was gone. The water sparkled, the sky shone sea blue. She would stay out here all day and go home tomorrow. "And what will I tell Charlie Wind? I know. I will say I saw the serpent, heard talking animals and danced with the little people." She listened to the stiff saw grass scratch the side of her boat. "If he thinks a lily is a lightning bolt, then I will tell him the wind is an animal god who talks." She thought better of that.

"No, I'm not going to lie. I'll stay here until I hear and see something . . . even"—she felt the tears rising—"even if I have to miss all of the Green Corn Dance festival."

y midmorning she had poled out of the saw grass and into Lost Dog Slough. This was a natural channel, a river within a river. Here the water flowed a bit more swiftly. The saw grass could not grow in it for the water ran deep. Even her pole would not touch bottom. She picked up the paddle and gently moved the boat along.

Water lilies bloomed pertly at the edges of the slough and underwater plants made forests below the surface. Billie Wind leaned over the side of the boat and watched schools of two-inch mosquito fish swim along trails in the submerged forests. One little fish swallowed a mosquito larva that was wriggling toward the surface for air. A long-nosed garfish swallowed the mosquito fish.

"And who will eat you?" she asked the garfish.

"Bulldozers, canal diggers and nuclear bombs," she answered, quoting her father and her teacher at the Kennedy Space Center School. "Then people will move to another planet, a planet that the spaceships will find circling another sun. Five-course dinners will grow on trees and there will be beds of orchids to sleep on. Medicine men will be scientists and children will be born knowing everything." She dreamed of the faraway planet and poled on into the wilderness.

When she could no longer see Lost Dog Island on the flat horizon she leaned back to rest. Her shoulders struck something hard. Putting down the paddle she reached back and pulled out a deerskin pouch that had been tucked into the tip of the stern. It belonged to her mother, Mamau Whispering Wind. Billie Wind smiled to see it, for Mamau like herself was realistic. Charlie Wind would wave white heron feathers over her boat for good luck, but her mother would give her tools and food to make certain her journey was safe.

The pouch contained two generous pieces of smoked venison, a loaf of cornbread, coconut meat, a machete for cutting down brush and a magnifying glass with which to start fires. Under the machete she found one of the string hammocks Whispering Wind could make so well, and beneath it her own sneakers and leather leggings. She would need them if she had to walk any distance in the cutting saw grass.

"Mamau Whispering Wind is a good thinker. She knows I could get lost or have an accident out here, so she's taken precautions." As she checked her hip pocket for her penknife, she saw that a fish spear had been tucked under the seat in the bow of the dugout.

"Dear Mamau Whispering Wind," she said. "You are my three white heron feathers."

She picked up the paddle again, dipped it into the smooth water and paddled on and on down the glistening pa-hay-okee.

The dugout slipped over the surface, riding high and quietly like a leaf. The breeze died down, the air warmed toward ninety degrees Fahrenheit, and the heat became an ominous presence that stifled even the movements of the birds. They stopped feeding and sought the shade of the distant tree islands. On the other hand, the mosquito wrigglers changed into winged adults in the glorious heat and arose from the surface of the water like smoke. Instantly they were pursued by squadrons of bomber-shaped dragonflies, who gobbled them up.

The snakes liked the hot temperature. They slithered through the water, hunting delicacies. They moved swiftly, one after another, on both sides of the boat, their pointed heads above water, making ripples.

"There are an awful lot of snakes out here," Billie Wind finally said to herself. "And they all seem to be moving west to east across Lost Dog Slough. And that's strange."

And the alligators were restless. On other trips down the slough, she had seen them hang quietly at the surface, eyes jutting above the water, watching and waiting for food. Today they were zigzagging beneath the surface of the water. She did not know why. Probably because it was hot, so hot in fact that she finally pulled her black hair over her face to make shade and stopped exerting herself. She lay back in the dugout and let the current carry her.

She drifted only a few feet a minute, for the water of the Everglades creeps. It is a slow river. Once, it seeped out of Lake Okeechobee, before canals were dug to drain the land south of the lake for farming. Now the river comes from rainfall only. It is one hundred miles long and seventy-five miles wide and ends in Florida Bay.

Drifting down the river of grass, Billie Wind could see the sun and the water and soils at work. Flowers bloomed before her eyes. Butterflies drank the nectar of the flowers and red-winged blackbirds ate the butterflies. The snakes ate the blackbirds and the alligators ate the snakes. Charlie Wind was right, all life came from the sun and the water and the soil and the air.

Just before noon the first clouds of the day formed on the horizon. They were small, the size of sheep. Billie Wind watched them gather and grow into mountainous billows that cast shadows on the saw grass, turning it from copper green to purple-brown.

A large mud turtle surfaced near her boat, took a breath and submerged. He swam laboriously toward the east with the snakes and alligators.

"See, Charlie Wind," she said. "Here beside me is the spirit of the turtle. He is beautiful but he does not speak."

A large-mouthed bass came close to the surface and paused. Grasping her spear she stood over him, thrust and missed. The spear shot down into the water and then popped up, for the stem was bamboo, and its joints were filled with air. She scooped up the spear and practiced on a floating leaf. Spearing fish was not as easy as her father made it appear to be.

The sounds of the glades were strange this day. Squawks, screams, croaks and pipings floated across the humid air. As she listened and dozed, her mind wandered back to the Space Center, where she and her brother had spent two winters with their father, Iron Wind. Mary had chosen not to go to school at the Space Center while Iron Wind worked on the launcher for the Voyager spaceships that explored the planets. So she did not know about astronomy and the quest for life in space. She knew only of serpents and talking animal gods and dwarfs.

And Mary had not heard Iron Wind when he said to Billie one evening in their trailer home: "We may need to move off the Earth someday. We are polluting this planet with chemicals and radiation from atomic weapons and nuclear reactors. Mankind is forcing mankind out into space to find another planet."

When Iron Wind worked at night Billie would wait for him outside the Space Life lab, staring up at the stars and wondering which one had a sapphire-blue planet with an Everglades and a girl like herself looking out toward her.

The dugout bumped into a clump of alligator flags, tall plants with single leaves growing like flags atop the bare stems. The plants got their name from these leaves and the fact that they usually surrounded alligator pools. Taking heed of this, she paddled around the plants into a clump of willows, drifted past the willows and came upon an alligator trail she had never seen before. She stood up to better see where it led. The trail wound for miles across the glittery pa-hay-okee to a green island. The island's dark color told her that it was a "hardwood hammock," not an island of willows or even of cypress trees like Lost Dog Island, but an island that grew mahogany and gumbo-limbo trees. There would be live oaks and bustic trees on the hammock as well as royal palms and pond apples. It was a wild island—unlike Panther Paw, which was planted to oranges, coconuts, papayas and corn. The limestone on the island would be pitted with sinkholes, deep wells leached by the acids from the plants. Orchids and ferns would festoon the trees and the floor of the forest, and its glades would be damp and cool.

"That's where I will spend the night," she said. "If any animal is going to talk, he'll talk to me there on that wild, natural island."

Billie Wind poled along the alligator trail. It wound and twisted through the reeds, crossed sloughs, then beelined through the saw grass for many miles.

The white clouds became purple thunderheads. They roiled and flashed with lightning. For the first time in almost two years she hoped they would not pour down rain although the glades needed it. The water was so low in places that the mud of lime and plant cells, called marl, was cracked and dry, and the saw grass that grew in it was withered. The only water in many places was in the alligator holes and trails, and some of these had now gone dry. Not far from Panther Paw a gator hole had dried up, sending the great reptiles down into the marl to estivate, to go into a protective sleep as some animals do in hot, dry weather.

She poled into an area where there were only a few feet of water in the deeply cut alligator trail. The boat stopped. She walked to the bow, put her pole in the marl, hung on to it, kicked the boat forward and dropped back into the stern. In this manner she moved slowly across the blazing glades.

A thunderhead flashed with lightning. She looked up.

"Are you going to rain?" she asked the clouds by way of testing the voice of the thunderbird god. "Answer me!" A clap of thunder banged overhead with such force that she jumped. "I'm sorry. I'm sorry," she called. "I believe you are there. I believe you are there." Then she grinned.

bout a hundred yards from the island she stopped poling and blinked both eyes. The island had disappeared. Was the swamp playing mysterious tricks on her? She shivered and stood up. The island returned to view six feet above the horizon line.

"Mirage," she said taking up the pole again, but she was unconvinced. The heat was not dry enough for a mirage. She moved forward gingerly, then a cloud passed over the sun and the island dropped to its proper place.

"If I didn't know better, I would say it was Charlie Wind scaring me with magic from the snake fang."

The island rose again, and although she knew there was some reasonable answer for the phenomenon she could not fathom it. A hot wind blew against her face. She gasped, for it was so intensely hot that she expected to see a rocket low overhead. Nothing was to be seen.

The wind changed; a cooler breeze nudged her face, and she headed for a small beach under a cabbage palm.

Out of the water rose a tail so large it could have belonged to a whale. It was sheathed in heavy armor and spiked with sharp ridges. The monstrous tail came straight toward her. She dropped to the bottom of the dugout as a mammoth alligator struck the stern of the boat and catapulted it forward. It rocked, tipped, but not quite over, then hit the beach with a crack. Billie Wind jumped ashore as a fifteen-foot alligator slammed his jaws closed on the rear of the boat. The wood splintered.

"Yo! yo!" She jabbed her pole at the monster. He grunted, spat out the wood and sank beneath the surface of the water.

A boiling turbulence marked his flight to the bottom of the moat that surrounded the island. The moat was maintained by the alligators who weeded and dug it deep with their mouths and tails. They pushed the debris ashore, leaving the water sparkling and clear. For their efforts the fish and turtles multiplied, and they ate their abundant crop.

Shaking from the scare, she pulled the dugout up on the shore, saw that the damage was slight and tied it to the cabbage palm. She threw her deerskin pouch over her shoulder, pushed back the limbs of a shrub and stepped into a hauntingly beautiful forest.

Gwad! someone screamed.

HO, HO, HO, HOHO.

Crank.

Billie Wind cast her eyes around the dim forest. Tree trunks were gnarled totems. Their limbs were draped with shrouds of Spanish moss. Some were homes to air plants and ferns.

Gwad. The screamer flashed through the trees and Billie Wind let out her breath.

"Woodpecker."

Crank.

"Wood ibis." She liked playing the game and laughed. "They do sound like people," she mused to herself. "I guess that's what Charlie Wind means when he says that the animal gods talk.

"But that isn't talk; not really."

Git! Git! Git!

"Or is it? Is that crazy anhinga, that snake-necked water bird, telling me to get out of here?" She walked slowly.

"There is something strange here. The air? the silence? the deadly smell?"

 few feet into the forest she came upon a cocoplum bush laden with plumlike fruits. She paused and popped the tart fruits into her mouth, then wended her way through a valley of ten-foot-high conte ferns and found herself in a mossy glade. Its odor was fresh with the smell of growing things. Nearby an enormous strangler fig dropped cascades of roots from its limbs, forming corridors and caverns.

Ho!

"*Ho*, yourself, Chief Barred Owl," she called, pleased to know what he was.

"If that is talk, then I'm an owl, too. *HO, HO, HO-HOHO!*" Presently a dark form came toward her through the gloom. The owl was approaching on flight feathers that made no sound. He swept up to a limb directly above her and folded his soft wings to his body. He swung his head from side to side, trying to identify the owl that he had heard. He bobbed his head up and down to better hear her sounds.

"Hello," she said. "I am a person. You came because you thought I was an owl.

"I can hoot your language, but you can not speak mine."

She crossed the glade to a cluster of strap ferns with their long thin leaves, pushed past them and came upon a circle of soft lichens and moss. She swung her pouch to the ground.

"This is my magic spot. I will sleep here and listen to the animals talk."

She selected two trees about six feet apart, from which she would sling her hammock, and was pulling it from her pack when she heard a strange wind.

She stood up. It whined like something alive.

"But it isn't a bird or a beast." Curious, she wended her way among vines and figs, across the island toward the sound. Pushing back the shoreline bushes she looked out on the endless expanse of saw grass prairie. There was no water gleaming in it. The blades were brown and dead. Gray clouds rolled and billowed.

"Rain," she cheered. "It really *is* going to rain. These clouds are not teasing." As she ran back to gather up her possessions she kept an eye out for a shelter. A deep sinkhole that looked like an open well caught her attention. It was almost fifteen feet deep and wide "and probably has caves in it, as most sinkholes do," she said as she let herself down a few feet to a ledge in the pit.

Below she saw her reflection in a pool.

"Water. That's good. Water erodes caves." Another ledge lay below the first and she dropped to that. From there it was an easy scramble to the bottom of the pit, where a huge log lay half submerged in the pool. She stepped upon it, bent down and peered into a cave.

"Lucky me," she said aloud. "See there, Charlie Wind, I didn't need three white heron feathers." She leaped from the log into the cave. The sandy floor was pocked with the inverted funnels of ant lions. The little insects sit at the bottom of these funnels that are really traps, waiting for traveling ants to slip and slide down. The pits are pitched at such a steep angle the ants can not climb out. They fall prey to the little killers.

"The ant lions tell me something," she said. "They build pits only in dry places; so this cave is dry. That's good."

She returned to her possessions and, slinging the pouch over her shoulder, hurried toward the pit. A deer, ears back, eyes wide with fright, bolted across the mound and ran full speed for the far side of the island where her dugout was beached.

"What's the matter with you?" she called to the deer. "Is the storm that bad?" The deer was silent. "Please talk," she called facetiously.

A marsh rabbit bounded over the ferns, running full out for the far side of the island. He zigged and zagged as rabbits do to confuse an enemy.

The barred owl took off toward the east, and overhead, a flock of wood storks frantically winged in the same direction. They squawked as they kept in touch with each other.

"What's going on?" she called to them. "Let Charlie Wind be right. Speak. Tell me why all the animals are frightened."

ardly had she spoken than she was struck by a blast of hot air, more searing than the one she had felt in the boat. It smelled of burning grass. And then she knew; she knew why the animals ran and why the island seemed to rise.

"Fire," she gasped. "This is no thunderstorm. The prairie is burning."

Now she could see flames through the trees. Running to the shore, she pushed back the limbs and looked out. Orange blazes licked the sky like serpents' tongues. They shot downward and devoured the grass. They spat black smoke as the many-tongued beast came rushing toward Billie Wind.

"The boat!" She turned and ran. Near the pit she thought better of escaping in the dugout. "I can't paddle hard enough. The fire is coming too fast."

The cave was her only hope. Letting herself over the edge of the sinkhole, she clambered down to the log, jumped into the water to wet herself down so she would not burn, and ran into the cave. She looked up.

Yellow and red fireballs shot through the trees. A live oak burst into flame; a mahogany tree shimmered in the heat, then exploded in fire. Billie Wind had seen all she wanted to see. Creeping deep into the cave, she hugged her calves and dropped her head onto her knees.

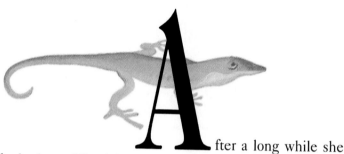

After a long while she looked up. The island was a fire box. Green limbs came to a boil and exploded like bullets. Flames ran up and around the trees like slithering serpents: millions and millions of them. A burning limb fell into the pit, struck the water, hissed like a snake and went out.

A deer screamed.

Fires in the Everglades are necessary. Billie Wind knew this. They burned seedling trees out of the pa-hay-okee so that only grass would grow. They thinned out the underbrush on the islands, and because the fires were frequent, they never became hot enough to burn the island trees. Hardwood hammocks like the one Billie Wind was on were protected by moisture from the plants, and they rarely if ever burned. The fires were simply not hot enough to penetrate them. And this had gone on for twenty thousand years. Then the practical white man fought and put out the Everglades fires. The underbrush grew dense and thick. Now, when fires start in the glades they burn hot, and they sweep through the islands, killing the trees and burning down into the rich humus.

The fire that roared above Billie Wind glowed like a blast furnace. It created rising winds that carried sticks and limbs high into the sky.

Inside the cave Billie Wind watched uneasily as flaming limbs dropped from the smoke clouds into the pit. A turtle plunged off the rim and splashed into the water. Lizards dropped like rain from the hot trees, and an armadillo, North America's relative of the sloth, crept to a ledge. His armored back was singed and sooty. He lifted his head, slipped and fell ten feet into the water. He did not come up.

Snakes slithered down the wall of the pit. Billie Wind counted more than a dozen before she lowered her eyes and curled up in a ball to sleep. She could not.

She wondered if her tribe could see the fire, and if so, would they try to rescue her?

"They won't," she remembered sadly. "I was curious once too often. Mary will tell them I went south down Lost Dog Slough instead of west. They will not look for me. They will think I am safe. Fires burn as the wind blows. This wind is from west to east."

She lay very still watching the reflected flames dance in the water and listening to the crackle and roar of the fire.

"Charlie Wind," she said after a long while, "there *is* a serpent."

An hour before dawn, Billie Wind, who had not slept all night, lifted her head and looked up at the fire. It still raged. She pushed farther back in the cave. As she moved, her hand struck something hard and round. She brought it close to her face for inspection. It was a clay bowl.

"Burial ground," she said. "This is a burial ground of the Seminoles. I should not be here." Nervously she went to the entrance and held the bowl in the light of the fire shining down from above. Around its rim were feathery drawings. Her fingers ran lightly over the coils of clay that formed the dark bowl. It was gritty to her touch. The grittiness was typical of bowls fired in sand by the ancient Indians.

"Calusa," she said. "This is a Calusa pot." She glanced around the cave. "This place is very old; very, very old. The Calusas were killed off four hundred years ago.

"And it is not a burial ground. Burial pots are broken to let the spirits out.

"Someone lived here. Some ancient ancestor lived in this cave." The light flared up and she crawled around the room on hands and knees curious to see and learn. Near the far wall she found a conch shell. A hole had been drilled through it, and the tough, thick lip had been ground to a sharp edge.

"A pick," she said. "Hey, ghostly ancestor, you had a pick. Who were you and why were you down

B·53

here in this cave?" She rocked back on her heels and saw that there was a long niche chipped into the wall.

"A bed." She climbed into it, stretched out and discovered that her head and feet touched the walls. "The ancestor was not much taller than I," she observed; then a thought occurred to her. She felt for human bones. To her relief she found none. "You did not die here," she said aloud. "You lived, and so will I."

As the sun came up the mood of the fire changed. The crackle and roar became a soft hum. The mist of morning was drifting across the island and seeping down into the pit. The air smelled of smoke and tree resin. Billie Wind coughed, took off her shirt and dipped it in the water. She held it over her nose and mouth to filter out the smoke. Lying on her belly, facedown, she breathed the heavy, cold air that still lay along the floor of the cave.

As the morning waned, the smoky mist vanished, leaving the air almost fresh. Billie Wind removed her filter, sat up and breathed deeply. A new sound was on the wind. It was a hiss, and beyond the hiss a splat.

"Rain!" she cried. "Mamau Whispering Wind, I hear rain. I'm all right. I'm all right."

Taking off her leggings and sneakers, clutching the bowl to her chest, she climbed into the bed of the ancient person and lay down. She closed her eyes and this time she did sleep.

Thinking About It

1. Billie Wind goes alone into the Everglades on a personal mission to understand the beliefs of the Seminole people. Think of something about your heritage that you would like to understand better. How will you go about learning it?

2. Billie Wind does not believe in the spirits of nature so she is not aware of what nature is telling her. What warnings of a fire did nature give her?

3. Only nature surrounds Billie Wind as she paddles into the Everglades, but a crowd surrounds Maniac Magee as he tries to undo the knot. What would happen if they switched places?

Another Book About Fires in Nature
Yellowstone Fires, Flames and Rebirth by Dorothy Hinshaw Patent describes the forest fire that burned almost one million acres of Yellowstone National Park in 1988 and the effects it had on the forest.

LAURENCE YEP

VIRTUE GOES TO TOWN

from <u>The Rainbow People</u>

After Virtue had buried his parents, he went to see the wise woman. "They say you can read a face like a page in a book. Tell me what my destiny is."

But the wise woman just kept sipping her tea. "What would you have? A quiet, happy life as a farmer? Or a life of sorrow and glory?"

"I hate being bored," Virtue said.

The wise woman studied his face a long time. She patted his shoulder sadly. "Then go into town."

When Virtue arrived there, he saw a long line of men. "I heard that town folk did the oddest things. Are you all practicing to be a fence?" he asked.

A townsman leaning against a wall looked at Virtue and then looked away again. But Virtue's voice was loud, and he was such a pest that the townsman finally said, "They're hiring workers, Turnip."

"The name's Virtue. And they can sign me up too. I left the farm to see the world and get rich." He got in line behind the townsman.

However, it was a hot, summer day and Virtue quickly became impatient. As he wiped at the sweat on his forehead, he shouted, "Hey, can't you go any faster?"

The foreman sat at his table in the shade. He ignored Virtue and went on just as slowly as ever.

"Hey, we're not getting any younger," Virtue yelled.

Still the foreman ignored him.

"Maybe he's deaf." Virtue started forward.

The townsman stuck out his arm. "Hey, Turnip, wait your turn."

"I told you. My name's Virtue. So why don't I just take you right with me, friend?" Virtue tucked his arm into the townsman's. The others were too afraid to say anything else, but everyone watched as he stomped up to the foreman.

"I can outplow a water buffalo and can harvest more than twenty folk," Virtue said.

The foreman took an instant dislike to Virtue. "You may be strong; but you're not that strong. No one likes a braggart."

"It's not bragging if you really can do it," Virtue said.

The foreman grunted. "I'm the boss here. I say how we do things. Get back there."

"Come on, friend." With a sigh, Virtue carried the townsman back to the end of the line.

It took most of the day before Virtue finally reached the table. Virtue made a muscle for the foreman. "No job's too hard for me."

The foreman put down his brush and folded his

hands over his big belly. "I have all of my work crew already. All I need is a cook. Can you do that?"

Virtue frowned. He thought a cook's job was beneath him, but times were hard and jobs were scarce. "Can I cook?" Virtue said. "I could cook a whale and fricassee a dragon."

The foreman twiddled his thumbs. He would have liked to turn Virtue away, but he needed a cook. "You only have to cook rice, dried fish and vegetables. I guess even you couldn't ruin that."

"Whatever I do, I always do well," Virtue promised. "I would make a better worker. But if you want me as a cook, then I'll be the best cook I can be."

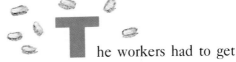

he workers had to get up at sunrise, but Virtue had to get up even earlier to boil the water for their tea. Even so, he always had the tea poured and the cold rice served in bowls before the first man was up. He tried to have a friendly, cheerful word for each of the other workers. "Smile, friend," he would say to one. "We're keeping farm hours now—not town hours."

And to another, he would say, "We're all in this together, neighbor."

And to a third, he would grin. "Teamwork. That's how we do it on the farm."

But all the other men were from town. They never thanked him. In fact, they never spoke to him. Behind his back, they laughed and called him the loud-mouthed turnip.

Still, Virtue did not give up easily. "These townsfolk will come around once they get to know me."

At noon, he served them supper. Then, picking up a huge cauldron in each hand, he went down to the river. Each of the cauldrons could have held a half dozen men, but Virtue dipped them into the water and lifted them out as easily as if they were cups.

After making several trips, he would set the cauldrons of water on big fires. By sunset, they would be bubbling. When the work crew came back, they would wash before they sat down to eat their dinner.

But one noon, the other workers were delayed. Virtue got hungrier and hungrier as he smelled the food. Finally, he ate his bowlful of rice. Still, there was no sign of anyone. Virtue was so bored that the only thing he could think of doing was to eat another bowlful of rice and wait.

When no one had shown up yet, he began to feel sorry for himself. "I do my job, but no one appreciates me. So maybe I'll just have another bowlful. That'll show them."

When he had finished his third bowl, he looked at the cauldron simmering on the big fire. "This rice is going to get burned. I shouldn't let it go to waste." Bored and lonely, Virtue began to eat right from the cauldron. Before he knew it, he had finished the whole cauldron of rice.

Tired and dirty, the work crew finally came back to camp. They were angry when they found the empty cauldron. "Where's our food, Turnip?" they demanded angrily. But no one went too close to Virtue.

Virtue gave an embarrassed cough. "My name's Virtue."

They glared at him. "You're nothing but a big sack of wind. How do you expect us to work on empty bellies?"

Virtue brightened. "Since I ate all your lunch, let me do all your work. It's only fair."

The foreman got ready to fire Virtue. "One person

couldn't meet our goals by himself."

"We take turns back on the farm. I'll do their work and they can do mine," Virtue said.

"You'll kill yourself," one of the work crew objected.

The foreman thought for a moment and then smirked. "Let him."

So Virtue left the others back in camp and marched off to work with the foreman. The foreman set a hard pace, but Virtue did not complain. By the end of the day, he had done all the work and more—much to the surprise of the foreman.

hen Virtue came back, he shook his head when he saw the one pot of hot water. "You're supposed to have hot water for me. That wouldn't wash a cat's tail." And then he saw the pot of rice they had cooked for him. "I've done the work of twenty men. I've got the hunger of twenty men. That wouldn't even feed a mouse."

"We don't have enough firewood," one of the work crew said.

"Then I'll take care of it myself this time." Picking up an ax in either hand, he marched up to the nearest tree. In no time, he had chopped it into firewood. Then, taking the huge cauldrons, he went down to the river and filled them.

One cauldron he used for his rice. The other he used for his bath.

When he finally sat on the ground, he wolfed down the whole cauldron of rice. The others just watched in amazement. Virtue laughed. "I work hard, I eat hard, friends."

All this time, the foreman had been thinking.

"You're not just bragging. You really can do the work of a whole crew." The foreman still didn't like Virtue, but it was more important to get the job finished. "Tomorrow you can do the work again."

But Virtue had learned a few things since he had left the farm. He winked at the rest of the crew. "We're all a team." He turned back to the foreman. "You're not going to fire them, are you?"

The foreman had been planning to do that very thing. Then he could pocket all the extra wages. But there was something in Virtue's look that made the foreman think again.

"No, they can be the cooks," the foreman said grudgingly.

One of the work crew grinned at Virtue. "No one will ever mistake you for a modest man, but your heart's in the right place." Then he bowed his head to Virtue. And one by one, the others did too.

And that was why there was only one worker but twenty cooks.

And even though Virtue went on to become a mighty warrior and general, he never lost his talent for making friends . . . and enemies.

THINKING ABOUT IT

1. Virtue always does the best he can at whatever he tries and usually does it better than anyone else. What can you do better than most people? Why are you better at it than most people?

2. Virtue is not just a name. Based on the story, how would you define *virtue?*

3. Use the hint in the last paragraph. Take Virtue on his next adventure. After all, no story really ends.

LAURENCE YEP

Explorers in a Different Country

FROM THE STAR FISHER

I t is 1927 and fifteen-year-old
Joan Lee has just arrived in West Virginia from Ohio. Here her
Chinese-American parents plan to open a laundry business in an
old schoolhouse that will also be their home. The long train ride,
new setting, and unfriendly townspeople are among the challenges
faced by Joan and her younger brother, Bobby, and sister, Emily.

When we had finished our supper, we helped
Mama unpack, which helped take our minds off the
day's events.

There was something exciting about moving into a
new house—as if we were explorers in a different
country. And this house was more unusual than most,
with high ceilings and walls with old, angular mark-
ings from the paintings, charts, and chalkboards they
had once borne.

In the very front of the building, Papa had finished
knocking together a crude counter, though the sten-

ciled sides of the wooden scraps needed to be painted over, and there were shelves behind the counter. In the next room, Papa had already set up two ironing shelves out of wooden planks; and we got out the irons, the watering bottles, and the starch while Mama set up her pedal-run sewing machine.

The third room was for drying, so Papa had strung clotheslines back and forth. There was more rope up than he had ever used in Ohio—as if he expected more laundry. Above the lines strung in even rows, far out of reach, was the tall ceiling with the molding. Desks and chalkboards had long since been carted away, but we could see the marks on the floors and the walls. And though the rooms had been washed and dusted, they still smelled of chalk and glue. A wood-burning stove squatted in one corner like a squat black bug. I supposed the school hadn't been fully converted to gas and the stove had been kept to heat the classroom in the winter. In Papa's methodical way, he had stacked kindling and wood beside it, ready to dry all the loads of laundry that would come.

The room next to the kitchen room was the washing room, where the wringing machine was already assembled. With a hammer, Mama opened the crate, and we unpacked the heavy laundry soap and the rest of our things. Then we ranged the washboards out like soldiers, preparing for the great battle the next day against the forces of filth. Papa had told me one time that the washboard was a Chinese invention that we had brought to America, though I don't know about that. Beneath the windows sat the row of big metal washtubs, gaping like so many empty frogs.

"Ah, here it is," Mama said. From one crate she brought out a small brass bell covered with flowery decorations and mottos in Chinese. We followed her in a procession back to the front door.

Papa had already prepared the hook over the door-way. I picked up Emily in my arms, and when Mama had given her the bell, Emily hung it up so that when the front door opened, it would make the bell ring. "Now we're really settled in," Emily said.

As the sun set, Mama began to turn on the gas jets in the house. They were little pipes that stuck out of the wall. When you lit them, the gas burned, giving off light.

In the kitchen next to the washing room, we finished taking the rest of Mama's things out of the crates, including the rice and some salted vegetables. "Now we can eat real food tomorrow," Mama declared.

When we had done what we could downstairs, I got the bags that Emily and I had been carrying and took them upstairs.

Together, four of us put together the bed that Emily and I used and placed it next to the window. Our dresser was already there, with the cracked mir-ror in the frame above it. Next to it was a chair. In our old home, our things pretty well crammed the tiny room we had. But everything looked a bit lost in that classroom.

Mama sent Bobby off to bed while she and I helped Emily get into her night-clothes. As she brushed out Emily's hair, Mama turned Emily toward the gaslight and pointed mean-ingfully toward it. "Remember, play with the gas jet and the gas might come into the house and choke you or blow up the whole house—and you'll get back to Ohio even sooner than you want."

Then, as she put us to bed, she told us a couple

of stories about children who had played with the gas jets and died particularly gruesome deaths.

As she tucked the quilt up around our necks, she looked down at Emily sternly. "And," she declared, "it all happened because bad, bad children disobeyed their parents." She stroked the hair out of Emily's eyes. "Now good night."

Mama went over to the gas jet and pointed at it again. "What did I say about these things when we lived in Ohio?" she asked Emily.

Emily would have kept a stubborn silence if I hadn't elbowed her. "Only you and Joan and Papa can turn it off," she mumbled.

With a nod of her head, Mama turned down the gas jet so that the light went out. When Mama was gone, I felt Emily's bony elbow in my side. "Joan?"

"What?" I mumbled sleepily.

Emily was lying on her side, looking at the wall where the gas jet was. "Do you think Mama would tell a fib?"

The pillow felt so soft at that moment that I just murmured, "She doesn't want you to play with the gas jets. Now good night."

As we lay there, I could hear the old building talking to itself. Out in the hallway, old boards creaked. Something rattled in a room below. The bed shook as Emily turned toward me for protection, but she took in her breath so sharply that I made the mistake of asking, "What's wrong?"

In the dim light coming in from the street, Emily's eyes looked very wide. "There's a tree. I can see its shadow on the shade. It's got these long, bony arms that are moving." She clutched at me. "I think it's trying to get us."

"Don't look at it, then." Putting a hand to her shoulder, I shoved her over onto her back. She lay there for a moment and then announced, "This is even worse. Now I can't see anything. I can just hear it." When the wind made the tree branches beat against the window, Emily scurried under the quilt. "Now it's trying to get us."

"Emily, come out of there before you suffocate." Exasperated, I tried to drag the quilt back down from her head.

Emily, though, had a death grip on it. "If there are any monsters there"—her voice came muffled through the quilt—"you want someone big like Joan and not someone small like me."

It took both hands, but I managed to get Emily's head back into the open air. "Now, no more shenanigans," I scolded her. "Go to sleep."

When I lay back down again, the pillow felt as soft as ever. But it wasn't too long before Emily poked me again. I tried to push her away without looking and waved my hand vaguely in the air. "Go away."

"I don't like it here," Emily insisted.

"That's nice," I murmured drowsily.

"This place is worse than a jail. It's a trap." I tried to ignore her, but every now and then these little pronouncements would spout from Emily. "I keep hearing the tree moving." A moment later: "It's coming in." And after a minute: "Joan-ee, I can't sleep."

"I can," I mumbled.

"I'm scared," she complained. "The tree's moving."

"It's just the wind," I muttered into my pillow.

Emily snuggled up against me. "It's going to get us."

Once Emily's imagination got going, it was hard to stop it. With a sigh, I rolled over onto my side to look at her, but Emily had buried her head underneath the quilt again. "No, the tree sounds just like the ocean."

Emily lowered the quilt to stare at me accusingly,

"You've never been to the ocean."

"Neither have you, so how do you know it doesn't? Come on, we'll make like spoons." I rolled Emily over onto her side so that her back was to me. Then I held her against me tight. "If I tell you a story, will you let me sleep?"

"You're the best storyteller," Emily said, trying to butter me up.

I gave her a little shake. "Will you go to sleep?"

Emily started to lay out the conditions for the performance. "And I like the way you add all sorts of details and do different voices."

"Will you?" I demanded.

"Yes," she promised.

"A young farmer was walking along the road," I began.

"I like that one," Emily said. I knew she did because whenever Mama told it, she always fell asleep.

"It was late on a fine afternoon," I started again.

"A summer afternoon," she corrected me.

"It was late on a fine summer afternoon," I said, and Emily fitted herself contentedly against me from head to toe. "And he'd just been to a town and sold a basket of turnips."

"And he was going home," Emily prompted me.

I put my hand to her head and stroked her hair. "Hey, who's telling the story?" I teased.

"You are." Emily shifted her head to my arm, and I could feel her small body rise and fall as she breathed. She seemed to feel safe now in my arms. As Emily had told me one time, "You might be bossy, but you always make things okay."

As Emily lay there quietly, I found myself wishing that were true. "And he was going home when he heard a woman singing. He stopped dead in his tracks to listen because her song hung like a rainbow to the ears, a rainbow that glittered and twisted through the air like a snake dancing."

I kept my voice as gentle as my hand. In the mirror above the dresser, I could see Emily's eyelids begin to droop. "When the song ended, it almost broke his heart. 'No, don't stop,' he whispered. By now the sun had disappeared over the horizon, and the trees looked as black and massive as a wall of black iron."

Emily's eyes were closed, and so I kept my voice deliberately soft in the darkness. "As the moon rose slowly, the woman's voice soared in greeting, singing of riding the back of the wind all the way into the night sky where the stars wriggled and shimmered like schools of fish."

I closed my own eyes, feeling at peace. I forgot about the train ride and the man at the station and the men by the fence. "The moonbeams reached the forest by the road, so that the edges of the leaves were like silvery smiles, and the black branches seemed to wave and point to a narrow path. Still he hesitated by the road, for the forest was the sort of queer place where anything could happen and had happened."

As I spoke, I felt myself floating into the darkness just like the voice. . . .

He stood there uncertainly because he was a sensible man who always did the sensible thing. But then the beautiful voice spoke of swimming through the night and gathering the glittering stars, and he knew he had to find the woman who sang of such things. So, taking a deep breath, he plunged off the road and down the dark, winding path.

Bushes grew around a little clearing on the banks of the stream, and he hid in their shadow as he peeked through the branches. There, standing in the open, were three women, their faces turned toward the moon as if they were drinking its light like wine. Each was lovely, but the loveliest was the singer herself.

They were dressed in silken gowns—though the farmer could not decide what color they were because they seemed to change every moment. Around the women's shoulders were cloaks of golden feathers that rippled with a soft light of their own like the sunlight on the surface of a pond.

Hardly daring to breathe, the farmer crouched in the dark forest as they danced to the one woman's triumphant song, sweeping their arms as if they were already in the night sky fishing for stars.

However, though it was dark, the night air was still muggy and uncomfortable. So the lovely singer suggested that they take off their cloaks because they were too hot; and the others were only too glad to shed the cloaks, which lay like piles of gold at their feet. Then, relieved of a hot, heavy burden, they moved with lighter, quicker steps.

Finally, when they were thirsty from the dancing and singing, the three turned to the stream. The farmer should have run away from the magical creatures, or he should have sat in the dark until they were gone. But the singing was so delightful that it had made him foolish—so foolish, in fact, that he not only stayed but did a terrible thing.

He crept out of the bushes and across the clearing. While the women's backs were turned, he snatched up the precious cloak of the lovely singer. It was still damp and warm from her dancing. Clutching it to his chest, he darted back among the bushes and hid it among the roots of a tall tree.

When the women turned around, the farmer strode boldly out of the bushes. Gazing only at the singer who had so enchanted him, he asked, "Please, what's your name?"

With sharp, frightened cries, though, the women instantly bent and snatched up their cloaks. Throwing them about their shoulders, they spread their arms and immediately changed into golden kingfishers that rose, darting and weaving, up the silver beams of moonlight.

All of them, that is, except the singer. "Wait, wait," she called and held up her cloakless arms toward the sky. But her sisters were now only distant black specks against the moon.

"I just want to talk," the farmer said desperately. "I don't mean you any harm."

Tears in her eyes, the singer turned. "If you speak the truth, let me leave."

However, now that she stood right before him, he knew he could not let her go. "If you marry me, I'll give it back to you."

"I'm a star fisher," she pleaded. "I belong in the sky."

Despite all her arguments, the farmer coaxed and begged her to marry him; and though she did not believe the farmer, it was her only hope, so the star fisher reluctantly agreed. She accompanied the farmer to his village, where her beauty caused all the other villagers to murmur in wonder.

When they were married, she pressed him for her cloak. "I'll give it back to you soon," he said guiltily. "Just stay with me a little longer."

Though she now trusted him even less than before, she had no choice. She lived with the farmer, but she no longer sang or danced. She did not even look up at the sky but always kept her eyes upon the ground.

Instead, she searched for the cloak constantly. She hunted all around the house and in the fields and even left to go back to the forest clearing. However, her husband had already removed the cloak from the original spot and hidden it in a newer, better place.

Eventually, she bore the farmer a daughter. And at times during those years, the village would occasionally hear two birds singing sweet, lovely melodies at night. However, the birds did not sound like nightingales or any other birds the villagers had ever heard.

Ashamed, the farmer would cover his ears, for he knew they were his wife's sisters calling to her to return to them. There were times when he almost kept his promise and gave her back her cloak, but he would look at his wife and know that he could never willingly give her up.

And then one evening when the sisters began a sad tune, the infant daughter tottered outside in the courtyard to listen. Lifting her head, she began to sing with them.

Hastily the farmer hurried outside to quiet her, but she had already stopped to stare up at a golden feather drifting down. Laughing, she stretched one pudgy hand up for the shining feather; but she missed it, and instead it landed on her sleeve, where it instantly turned into a spot of blood. Frightened as much by the sight of blood as by the strangeness of the event, the girl began to scream in terror, waving her arm stiffly.

The farmer took the frightened child to their house, where his wife waited in the doorway. When she saw the spot of blood on her daughter's sleeve, she looked at the farmer and saw that he understood also: her sisters had marked the child as a star fisher.

Even so, the years went on. Her sisters sang, the farmer made promises, the star fisher hunted, and their daughter grew.

She could sing and dance, and in her the farmer found the sweet delight he had lost in her mother. And the farmer, afraid of the other star fishers, always kept his daughter close to home. If she ventured outside under her father's watchful eye, the other villagers avoided the half-magical child, whispering and pointing at her.

"I don't belong here," she had once complained to her mother.

"Neither of us does," her mother had sighed.

Finally the star fisher saw her chance and asked her daughter to play a game with her father; and when she cheerfully agreed, the star fisher coached her carefully on what she was to do.

That evening, she sang and danced in the courtyard for her father, as had become their custom; but after a while she stopped. When their father asked her what was wrong, she pretended to be frightened, saying that her mother had said she was going to leave him that evening.

His eyes automatically went to a pile of rice straw, but just as quickly he looked back at his daughter and assured her that her mother was only making a bad joke.

As she had been directed, she dutifully told her mother where her father had looked. That very evening, when he was asleep, the star fisher went to the heap of straw. With quiet desperation, she searched through the straw and then with her fingers clawed at the dirt beneath. There, sealed inside a box, was her magical cloak.

As she held it up, the feathers glimmered in the

B·76

moonlight as if finally waking after all these years. And the light woke her family, as it did all the villagers.

As her daughter stumbled sleepily into the courtyard, the star fisher turned triumphantly. "I'll come back for you."

"No, please, don't go," the farmer begged as he ran out into the courtyard.

The star fisher, though, simply threw the cloak about her shoulders and raised her arms skyward. In the wink of an eye, she had changed into a golden kingfisher that circled joyfully up toward the moon.

"Wait, wait," the farmer said as he held out his arms after her.

But the bird only soared higher until she vanished from sight. And suddenly, from deep within the night sky, her sisters welcomed her gleefully in song.

The villagers heard the birds only one other time, and that was when the mother returned for her daughter. And though the mother never came back, the daughter could sometimes be seen overhead at night, golden feathers shining in the moonlight as she glided over the long, winding Milky Way, skimming up the stars like a kingfisher scooping up a beakful of tiny, shining fish. And then, her body glowing with stars, she would sweep across the black sky like a fiery comet, back and forth, back and forth. . . .

Outside our window, the tree was still rustling. "I can hear the tree," Emily said sleepily, "but it doesn't sound scary anymore. It sounds just like the wind . . . through wings."

I said very softly, "And the star fisher would stretch her wings and let the wind lift her up, higher and higher, on and on . . . like an endless river flowing toward the moon. . . . "

And it was around then that Emily began to snore.

STARTING AT A PENNY A WORD

Laurence Yep

Laurence Yep

Sometimes kids ask me how I decided to become a writer. Originally, I wanted to go into chemistry because of a high-school chemistry teacher who made the subject fun. We learned electrical bonding, for example, by making explosives. I was less inspired by English class, but it was eventually my English teacher who shaped my career choice. In order to get an *A* in English, we had to get a piece of writing published. Although I never published anything in high school, I was bitten by the bug. I knew I would be a writer.

My first published piece was a short story in a science-fiction magazine titled *Worlds of If.* I received a penny a word! How did I come to write science fiction? I grew up playing with kids of African American heritage and attended school in Chinatown, so I had to approach white culture as something of a stranger. I read science fiction and identified with the isolated life and alienated heroes. Like those characters, I had to adapt in order to survive. When I began to write, it was natural to choose outsiders as subjects. I suspect that kids in the process of growing up today like horror stories and science fiction for the same reasons—to learn about how they can survive in a world that sometimes seems rather alien.

It was by accident that I started to write for young people. Years ago, a friend and editor (who later became my wife) asked me to write science fiction for kids. I soon learned that I liked writing for young people. I still do.

Dragons appear in many of my stories. I really believe there is a dragon in every one of us. Not a green scaly thing but something that represents creativity. Chinese dragons brought rain, making the crops grow. "Dragon" is a label for whatever it is in the unconscious that starts the creative process.

Where do the characters in these two stories come from? The title character in "Virtue" is like a family friend who had a "Can Do" attitude. But the story really comes from a Southern Chinese tale about a General Yang. Joan Lee in "Explorers in a Different Country" is based on my Auntie Mary, the storyteller of the family. Emily is based on my mother. There really was a family laundry in West Virginia, and my mother's face shines when she recalls her youth there. I visited their old neighborhood years later; the area had become suburban and the laundry-schoolhouse is now a bank parking lot.

These stories should provide readers with a way to understand a people and their dreams. Folk tales are strategies for living. They tell how to turn defeat into victory, disappointment into celebration. My own Aunt Mary was a storyteller who managed to combine warmth, cheer, and pragmatism in her own tales.

Thinking About It

1. Emily is comforted when Joan tells her a familiar story. Be Emily. Tell why the story comforts you.

2. Laurence Yep knows what it's like to be a stranger in a new place. Will the characters in "Virtue Goes to Town" and "Explorers in a Different Country" eventually fit in or will they always feel like strangers? What makes you think they will or won't?

3. The star fisher is a beautiful and magical creature. Think of a way to show your impression of the star fisher. You might choose a list of words, a poem, or a picture.

Gordon Parks

Skip Berry

Gordon Parks: Focus on America

It was a cold, clear January morning in 1942 when Gordon Parks stepped off the train in Washington, D.C.'s Union Station. Bags in tow, the 29-year-old photographer hailed a cab, his skin tingling with excitement at being in the nation's capital for the first time. He wanted to see the places where great statesmen had delivered the speeches and drawn up the legislation that had shaped the country's history. He wanted to walk where presidents had walked. But most of all, Parks wanted to take great pictures. After all, it was his skill with a camera that had earned him the chance to come to Washington.

Parks was still elated at having been awarded a fellowship by the Julius Rosenwald Fund, for it provided him with money for an entire year to study photography in the manner and place of his choice. The fellowship had enabled Parks to transform a longstanding dream into reality: to work for the highly regarded photography division of the Farm Security Administration (FSA), a branch of the federal government set up by President Franklin Roosevelt to help farmers suffering from the effects of the Great Depression. Photographers employed by the FSA were responsible for documenting life in America during the depression.

After dropping off his luggage at the rooming house where he would be staying, Parks hopped a streetcar and headed off to make history. He was the first—and as it turned out, the only—black photographer ever to work for the FSA.

On that January morning, Parks was exhilarated by the prospect of working for the FSA, not by the fact that he would be the initial black on its staff. A few years earlier, while working as a waiter in railroad dining cars, he had got his first inkling of the power of fine photography by studying magazine photos shot by such well-known FSA photographers as Jack Delano, Dorothea Lange, and Walker Evans. Their work had inspired his decision to make photography his career.

Parks got off the streetcar at the intersection of Fourteenth and Independence avenues. He stood for a moment in front of the large red brick building that housed the FSA, feeling the weight of the camera bag slung over his shoulder. This was the place he had left Chicago to find. Then, taking a deep breath, he pulled the front door open and went in search of the photography division.

As he wandered the corridors, Parks anticipated stepping into a room filled with photographs and fellowship. But when he finally found the door he was looking for, it opened instead into a room filled with nondescript office furniture and rows of file cabinets. There was not a photograph or a fellow photographer in sight. What was more, the windows were filthy.

"Welcome to Washington," cried a white-haired, bespectacled figure who bounded out of a nearby office, hand extended. "I'm Roy."

This was the man Parks had come to meet, the man who had invited the young photographer to Washington when he had expressed a desire to work for the FSA during his fellowship year. A legend among photographers, Roy Emerson Stryker had run the FSA's photography division since its formation. Though not a photographer himself, he had an unerring eye and a keen sense of the emotional impact of photos.

Under Stryker's guidance, many of the country's best photographers had contributed vivid, memorable images to the FSA's documentation of life during the depression years. By 1942, Stryker had compiled files full of some of the most important photographs in American history. Indeed, the FSA's photo collection was both a searing indictment of the greed that had laid land and lives to waste and a powerful testament to human misery and dignity in a trying time.

Parks had come to Washington to learn as much as he could about photography from Stryker; but the first thing his new teacher did was take his cameras away from him. "You won't be needing those for a few days," said Stryker, locking the battered Speed Graphic and the Rolleiflex in his office closet. Then he instructed his newest staff member to spend some time getting acquainted with the nation's capital. "Go to a picture show, the department stores, eat in the restaurants and drugstores," Stryker said. "Get to know this place. Let me know how you've made out in a couple of days."

Parks agreed to follow his new boss's orders, even

Three generations of
Yellowknife Indians sat for
this portrait in 1944.

though he thought they were a bit unusual. After all, he had come to Washington to learn everything he could, and if walking around the city doing what he pleased was Stryker's idea of a training exercise, Parks was all for it. Besides, he had been looking forward to exploring the city.

Parks decided to begin his day on the town by heading downtown for breakfast. Stopping at a drugstore, he went inside and sat on a stool at the counter, only to be accosted by an angry waiter. "Get off that stool," the man said. "Don't you know colored people can't eat in here? Go round to the back if you want something." Everyone in the place stared at Parks as he retreated to the sidewalk.

Perplexed by what had just happened, Parks set off down the street to try his luck somewhere else. He stopped at a hot dog stand, where the white-coated vendor served him, albeit reluctantly and rudely. When Parks tried to buy a ticket at a movie theater, something he had done in plenty of other cities around the country, he was refused admission. And when he entered a department store in search of an overcoat, none of its many idle salesclerks would wait on him. In 1942, racism seemed to be everywhere in Washington, D.C., from the corner drugstore all the way, as he eventually learned, to the halls of Congress, where southern congressmen were unhappy with Stryker for adding a black photographer to his staff.

Parks was both angered at and bewildered by the attitudes he encountered. Racial discrimination was not a new experience for him: He had been taunted and cursed at in towns and cities throughout the country—from his childhood home of Fort Scott, Kansas, to the streets of Chicago and New York. But finding it so blatantly displayed in Washington, D.C., was something he had not expected.

After a few frustrating hours, Parks returned to Stryker's office and demanded to have his cameras back. He would show the world, he declared, what the capital of the United States of America was *really* like.

Rather than give Parks his equipment, Stryker asked him to sit down and talk about his morning on the town. Parks poured out his disgust at how he was treated throughout the city.

"Whatever else it may be, this is a southern city," Stryker said after the angry young photographer had finished talking. "Whether you ignore it or tolerate it is up to you. I purposely sent you out this morning so that you can see just what you're up against."

Stryker went on to tell Parks that as the only black photographer in the FSA, he was going to encounter a variety of attitudes within the agency, especially among the lab technicians who processed the photographers' film and developed their prints. All of them are good technicians, Stryker said, but they are also all southerners. "I can't predict what their attitudes will be toward you," he told Parks, "and I warn you I'm not going to try to influence them one way or the other. It's completely up to you." He then escorted Parks throughout the FSA building, introducing him to various employees. Their reactions ranged from smiles and handshakes to abrupt nods and cold shoulders.

After the tour, Stryker gave Parks his first assignment. He asked him to write out his plan for fighting discrimination. You cannot just take a picture of a white salesman, waiter, or ticket seller and label him prejudiced, Stryker told him. After all, a racist looks like anyone else. The camera is only able to expose the true face of America by showing those people who have suffered at the hands of others. Your images will have an emotional impact only if you, the photographer, bring your own feelings to your pictures.

Stryker told Parks to put his experiences into words, then find ways to turn what he had written into pictures that expressed those experiences. "Think in terms of images and words," Stryker said. "They can be mighty powerful when they are fitted together properly." To help Parks get started, Stryker threw open a file drawer and told him to study the work of other FSA photographers.

Parks spent the next few weeks sifting through hundreds of photos, steeping himself in powerful images of the Dust Bowl, a region in the central United States devastated by intense drought in 1936. Its rural inhabitants, already gravely affected by the depression that began in late 1929, lost all sources of income from their farms. Battered by poverty, thousands of displaced Americans drifted down the Dust Bowl's highways in search of new lives. Along the way, many of them came within camera range, and their struggles to overcome the grim realities of the time became a central part of the FSA's record of the 1930s.

As moving as the photographs were, Parks found the written accounts that accompanied them equally provocative. Together, the photographs and texts formed a clear and detailed record of the period, dredging up all the human misery that resulted from environmental and economic hardship. Parks began to see just how potent the combination of well-conceived photos and a well-written essay could be. To portray racial discrimination, he had to do more than simply point a camera at the problem.

Parks got the chance to put into practice what he had just learned sooner than he expected. One evening, Stryker suggested that Parks strike up a conversation with the thin, gray-haired black woman who cleaned the FSA building. Parks shrugged at the suggestion, believing it to be another of his boss's odd notions; yet he decided to give it a try. He searched the woman out, then spent an awkward few minutes trying to make small talk with her.

Gradually, the woman began to discuss her life in earnest. Her mother had died when she was young, and her father had been lynched. Her husband had been shot 2 days before the birth of their daughter, who had died at the age of 18, just 2 weeks after giving birth to her second child. This woman was now trying to raise her two small grandchildren, one of whom was paralyzed, on the meager salary she earned mopping floors.

Unable to offer the woman any immediate help, Parks responded the only way he could think of at the time. "Can I photograph you?" he asked.

"I don't mind," she replied.

The result was a photo Parks later called "unsubtle," but one that ranks among his best-known works. Entitled "American Gothic, Washington, D.C.," it depicts the sharp-featured cleaning woman standing against a background of the American flag, a broom in one hand and a mop in the other.

During the following month, Parks continued to photograph the same woman in a variety of settings, including her home and her church. At the end of the month, he brought all of the photos to Stryker and spread them out for him to examine. Parks heard what he had already figured out for himself. "This woman has done you a great service," Stryker said. "I hope you understand this."

Parks did. Thanks to the cleaning woman, he was beginning to understand how demanding documentary photography could be. Stryker had set high standards

Gordon Parks took this
portrait of Flavio, a twelve-year-old
Brazilian boy, in 1961.

for FSA photographers: He expected them not only to get involved with their subjects but to have empathy for the people whose lives they were documenting. Yet a photographer should not let emotions interfere with the ability to present the facts of the story.

Parks also realized during his first month in Washington, D.C., that the demanding process of documentary photography was going to be even more difficult because he was black. Since its earliest days, photography had been a profession pursued predominantly by whites. No one was waiting with bated breath for the first great black photographer to appear.

Yet Parks had not forgotten what his mother had repeatedly told him while he was growing up in Kansas: "If a white boy can do it, so can you. Don't ever come home telling me you can't do this or that because you're black."

Thinking About It

1. Gordon Parks fights discrimination. Is there something that you feel strongly about or feel the need to fight against? How would you reveal your feelings to others and perhaps persuade them to agree with you?

2. When Gordon Parks was frustrated by the way he was treated on his first day in Washington, his new boss told him to put his experiences into words and then find ways to turn his words into pictures. How did the cleaning woman help Parks? How do the photos that appear in this selection express Parks's experiences?

3. If you were trying to find Gordon Parks today, where would you begin your search? What subjects might he be photographing?

In the 1880s, soon after her father's death, Elizabeth Cochrane and her mother moved to Pittsburg, Pennsylvania. (The final *H* was not added to Pittsburgh until 1911.) When Elizabeth wrote a letter in response to a newspaper column filled with unfair remarks about women, George A. Madden, managing editor, was impressed. He published an article she wrote and even asked her for other ideas.

WHO IS THIS NELLIE BLY?

*E*lizabeth Cochrane appeared fragile for her height of five feet five inches. She wore her chestnut-colored hair in a chignon with bangs, a youthful style in those days, and had a jaunty sailor hat on her head. In spite of the determined gleam in her wide hazel eyes, she had a meek and mild appearance. The *Dispatch*'s reporters, who shared the one big city room, didn't know what to think of her.

Newspaper offices in the nineteenth century echoed with the clatter of presses from the floors below. The rooms smelled of printer's ink, gaslights, and tobacco, and were filled with a haze of cigar smoke. Chewing tobacco was popular, too, and the men were often careless when they aimed at the spittoons. The floors were filthy. In Sally Joy's* city room in Boston, the more gentlemanly reporters put newspapers down so she wouldn't get her long skirts stained with tobacco juice.

Elizabeth Cochrane looked out of place in this setting. A more timid woman would have turned and fled, but her ladylike appearance masked a will of iron. She informed the gawking reporters, sitting at desks crowded together and piled high with copy paper, that Mr. Madden had sent for her. When they directed her to his desk, she introduced herself and said she had come with her ideas.

If George Madden was surprised by Elizabeth Cochrane's sudden appearance in his city room, he was shocked by the subject on which she wanted to write. Divorce, she told him, was an issue that needed to be discussed in the newspaper.

Elizabeth tried hard to persuade Mr. Madden to give her a chance. He protested at first, but finally agreed to let her prove she could do what she said she could. He sent her home to write her article on divorce, and probably thought he would never see her again.

Elizabeth, however, tackled her new project immediately. She had the notes on divorce cases that her father had made during his years as a judge, but she had been doing some research of her own as well. Since she and her mother had spent almost all of their inheritance from her father, they had changed addresses several times, each time selecting a less expensive place. By the time "What Girls Are Good

*A young woman who talked herself into a job as a reporter on the Boston *Post* when she was eighteen.

For"* was printed, they were living in rundown lodgings in a poor section of the city, where Elizabeth had talked to several women who had suffered because of unfair divorce laws.

*A*ll night long, Elizabeth worked on her article, writing and revising, scratching out passages and copying it over. At that time there were no word processors and no portable typewriters to make the work easier. Even in the newspaper offices, articles were composed with pen and ink. Despite the long, slow process, Elizabeth persisted until her story was just the way she wanted it. The next morning she returned to the *Dispatch* office with a final draft that was neat and easy to read. More importantly, the article said something. Mr. Madden was impressed and immediately agreed to publish the story.

George Madden was a businessman. He might have believed, as the article in his paper had said, that respectable women stayed at home until they married, or at worse went into a "woman's profession" such as teaching or nursing. Still, he knew the facts. Since the Civil War, women had been working in mills, factories, and offices. The thought of a woman in politics made him shudder, but a woman had run for president in 1884.

In spite of his doubts, Madden found himself encouraging Elizabeth Cochrane. If one thing could overcome his prejudices, it was the promise of a controversial series for his newspaper. Controversy

*An essay expressing ideas held by most men in the 1880s. The writer of the article called employment of women in business a threat to the national welfare.

The women in these photographs worked in a bottle factory in Pittsburgh, Pennsylvania, at the turn of the twentieth century.

increased a newspaper's circulation, and that was good business.

He asked for more stories, saying that if the series on divorce were a success, he would give Elizabeth a regular job and pay her five dollars a week. She accepted at once.

Madden had only one problem left. He was worried about allowing Elizabeth to use her own name. What would people say if they knew he had hired an eighteen-year-old girl to write on such a sensitive subject as divorce? What would her family say? She had respectable and old-fashioned older brothers who would not approve of her new career.

Just as Mr. Madden and Elizabeth Cochrane agreed to invent a pen name, Mr. Madden's assistant, Erasmus Wilson, began to hum a popular Stephen Foster song. Everyone knew the words:

> Nelly Bly, Nelly Bly,
> bring the broom along.
> We'll sweep the kitchen clear, my dear,
> and have a little song.
> Poke the wood, my lady love,
> and make the fire burn,
> And while I take the banjo down,
> just give the mush a turn.
> Heigh, Nelly, Ho, Nelly,
> listen love, to me;
> I'll sing for you, play for you,
> a dulcet melody.

From that day on, Elizabeth Cochrane was Nellie Bly, and Madden immediately published her articles on divorce. The subject alone was enough to make people sit up and take notice, but the newspaper-reading public of Pittsburg was just as intrigued by the author. Who was this Nellie Bly? they wondered.

The *Dispatch* made the most of the mystery surrounding its new reporter's identity. Circulation improved dramatically as Nellie wrote more articles. In time, she came up with an idea that would set the tone for her entire newspaper career—she asked Mr. Madden if she could write about life in the slums and factories of Pittsburg. As a reporter and a reformer, she would tell the real story of her own experiences visiting these places, from a lady's point of view. She would take an artist with her to sketch what she saw. Mr. Madden saw the circulation of the *Dispatch* going up and up . . . and agreed.

Nellie brought the broom along, as the song says, and set out to sweep Pittsburg clean. It needed it. Under smoke-blackened skies, which glowed flame red at night, workers were little more than slaves to uncaring factory owners. Women in a bottle factory worked fourteen-hour days in an unheated building. Children were endangered by living in dirty, disease-ridden, fire-prone buildings in a slum called the Point.

When Nellie Bly joined the staff of the *Dispatch*, more than 156,000 people lived in Pittsburg. Many were immigrants, drawn by jobs in the iron and steel industries. Few labor unions protected these unskilled workers, and no social service agencies existed.

Nellie brought her discoveries of social injustices to public attention through the *Dispatch*. She was not content to sit at her hard-won desk in the city room, letting others do the research. Every story was her own, from the first idea, through the investigation and writing, to her byline, or name, on the finished article.

A bottling factory was Nellie's first target. The glass industry was Pittsburg's third largest business; some seventy factories produced half the nation's glass, and more champagne bottles than there were in France. Accompanied by her artist, she located the factory owner and told him she wanted to write an article for the *Dispatch* about his factory. Deceived by her ladylike manner and pleasant smile, he welcomed her with open arms. He thought she was offering him good, free publicity, so he told her to talk to anyone and look anywhere.

Nellie talked to the workers as the artist sketched. Some of these women stood on an icy cement floor for fourteen hours at a stretch. To cope with the winter cold that seeped through the factory walls, the workers had to wrap rags around their feet, which kept their toes from freezing. Several hundred workers shared one toilet, along with a family of rats. Worse yet was the daily risk of injury from broken or exploding bottles. Since worker's compensation did not exist, an injury could result in the loss of a person's job and only source of income.

Nellie was shocked by the conditions in the factories, and she channeled all her outrage into print. She held nothing back, including names, dates, and drawings. When her article appeared in the *Dispatch*, every copy of that day's paper sold quickly at the city's newsstands.

The factory owners were enraged when they saw Nellie's articles. Letters flooded the *Dispatch* office. Although Nellie faced protests, and even threats, efforts at reform began which eventually improved conditions in the factories of Pittsburg.

*N*ellie attacked the slums next. In the course of her own frequent moves, she had seen how crowded many of the city's tenement buildings were. In the Point she found a family of twelve living in one unheated room. In the rickety wooden shanties along Yellow Row, and the ramshackle cottages on the hill at Skunk Hollow, Nellie Bly asked questions and got answers. When she wrote her story, she named the slumlords, hoping to shame them into repairing their buildings.

The uproar this time was even greater than it had been after her article about the factory. Pittsburg businessmen began to organize against the threat of Nellie Bly. They claimed she was ruining the city's reputation. Despite fourteen thousand chimneys that polluted the air, they still insisted that Pittsburg was one of the healthiest cities in the United States. In fact, they said that people worked so hard that they didn't notice the smoke. Pollution had killed the grass and flowers, but a child who complained about the foulness of the air was told she should be "grateful for God's goodness in making work, which made smoke, which made prosperity." With that kind of thinking, no wonder the businessmen threatened George Madden with the loss of all his advertising if he didn't stop those reform-minded articles by Nellie Bly.

George Madden's business sense told him it was time to let things cool down. He gave Nellie a raise to ten dollars a week and made her society editor for the *Dispatch*. Nellie Bly began writing about the upper classes, whose parties, art, drama, and books were part of a world far removed from the city's slums.

Plays, lectures, concerts, and charity balls soon left Nellie bored and restless. "I was too impatient," she wrote, "to work along at the usual duties assigned women on newspapers." Yet nearly a year passed before she could persuade Mr. Madden to let her write serious articles again.

A modern jail, Riverside Penitentiary of Western Pennsylvania, had just been built to replace the old Western Penitentiary. It was the most up-to-date facility of its kind, and Nellie wanted to visit it. Her

Steel mills, Pittsburgh, Pennsylvania

article would be full of praise, she argued. Why not let her cover its opening? Reluctantly, Madden agreed.

In her article, Nellie praised the new facility's separate cells for inmates and large common work and recreation areas, but she used this praise of one jail as a starting point to criticize the rest. When Madden read her attack on other Pennsylvania jails, he knew trouble lay ahead, but he decided to print the article anyway.

*M*eanwhile, Nellie wanted to take another look at the factories. This time she went undercover, dressing herself as a poor woman looking for a job. She was hired at the first factory where she applied, though she had no skills. Her job was to hitch cables together in an assembly line with other young women. They could be fined for talking, or even for smiling, but Nellie did manage to learn that they all suffered from headaches.

She soon understood why. The light was so dim that her head began to ache, too. Then her feet started to hurt, because she had to stand. Her hands became raw and started to bleed. Before long, she ached all over. Just like the workers in the bottle factory, these young women kept working in spite of their fear of blindness and the constant discomfort. They had to work to live.

The women's supervisor kept urging them to work faster and faster. He paced back and forth behind them, yelling out threats and foul language. Since Nellie had been brought up to have good manners, she found it difficult to listen to curses and insults for hours on end. Finally, Nellie simply walked away from the assembly line to get a drink of water.

The foreman fired her.

When Nellie's two stories appeared in the *Dispatch*, the response was overwhelming. The paper's sales increased, and Nellie was criticized by just about everyone. City law enforcement officials said she wasn't qualified to judge their jails. The clergy called her shameless for visiting a men's prison without a chaperon. Again, the factory owners and businessmen of Pittsburg threatened to withdraw their advertising. Madden raised Nellie's pay to fifteen dollars a week and sent her back to write the society page.

The other reporters of the *Dispatch* appreciated her, even if the targets of her articles didn't. "Only a few months previous I had become a newspaper woman," she wrote, and in October, 1886, she became the first woman invited to join the Pittsburg Press Club. She was not, however, given any more controversial assignments.

Then one day, Nellie Bly saw a picture of some Aztec ruins in an art gallery window. Suddenly, story ideas about Mexico tumbled one after another into her mind. Nellie believed she could write articles describing what she saw, as travelogues did, but she could add more substance to her stories.

As usual, Nellie's enthusiastic plans didn't impress her boss at the *Dispatch*. She couldn't go running off to Mexico alone, Madden protested. Mexico had an unstable government. Mexicans mistrusted foreign reporters, and she didn't even speak Spanish.

Nellie had an answer for everything. She would learn Spanish and travel with her mother. What could be more respectable? she asked. Besides, she would not be going as a reporter for the *Dispatch*—the trip to Mexico would be a personal vacation. Of course, if Mr. Madden wanted to buy any stories, she would be sending some back. . . .

THINKING ABOUT IT

1. As a reporter and a reformer, Nellie Bly told what things were like in the 1880s. As you read this selection, what did you learn about life in the 1880s?

2. Who was this Nellie Bly? Did the newspaper articles she wrote bring about reforms in her own time, or did the stories only create more problems? Be ready to support your argument.

3. If Nellie Bly came to your town today, what would she write about? Choose a topic that would interest her. Then tell her what she needs to know to write about the subject you've chosen.

JEAN FRITZ

What? Quit the Battle?

From Make Way for Sam Houston

All his life Sam Houston liked to do things in a big way or not at all. But when he was ten and eleven and twelve years old, there was nothing very big going on. The last battle of the American Revolution had been over and done with twelve years before he'd even been born. (He'd been born on March 2, 1793.) Life had settled down to a day-in, day-out affair except perhaps for those people who lived in the West. And Sam didn't. He lived in Virginia with his mother, his four older brothers, his younger brother, and his three little sisters. His father, who was in the militia, was sometimes at home but most times he was not.

Of course Sam could have gone to school, but he saw no sense in that. He could already read and he

PORTRAIT OF SAM HOUSTON

The State Capitol, Austin, Texas
William H. Huddle, 1888

This painting was done from a
photograph taken in 1857.

didn't like to be told how to hold his pen and where to put his margins and such foolishness. Besides, who ever heard of anything big happening in a schoolroom? Instead he pretended to do big things. Sometimes he took down his father's second-best sword and pretended to be a Revolutionary soldier, slashing down Redcoats. Sometimes he whittled. Chipping away at a soft piece of pine, he let his mind go loose and heroic. Most often he read hero stories. His favorite hero was a Roman, Caius Marius, who started out as an ordinary boy but grew up to be a famous general. Sam especially liked the picture in his hero book of Marius when he'd been exiled from Rome by his enemies. There he was, standing all alone in his bare feet among some African ruins, but did he look beaten? Not Marius. He held his head high and smiled as if he knew he'd win out in the end. That was the way Sam would stand if he ever found himself in such a fix.

Then one day when he was thirteen everything changed for Sam. His father came home and announced that they were moving to Tennessee. Of course Tennessee was not in the Far West, but it was in the right direction and for all Sam knew, it might be Hero Country. Sam's father sold their Virginia farm for 1000 pounds, bought a new wagon for the trip, and wound up his business affairs.

And then Sam's father died. But since the Virginia farm had been sold and there were 419 acres of land waiting in Tennessee, his mother told the boys to load up the wagons. They were going anyway. And before long they were off—a five-horse wagon in the lead, a four-horse wagon following, and a string of dogs lolloping along on either side.

As it turned out, Tennessee was a fine place, but all Sam was allowed to see of it was 419 acres of unplowed, unplanted land. Sam was fourteen now, old enough to do a man's work, his brothers told him. Indeed, they never stopped telling him. Do this. Do that. Come here. Get a move on. Every time Sam ran off to read his hero books, his four bossy brothers would drag him back.

After a while his brothers gave up on Sam. He just wasn't cut out to be a farmer, they decided, so they took him to Maryville, the nearest town, and put him to work clerking in a store. That was even worse. Now Sam was at the beck and call of everyone who came into the store. All day he had to weigh pota-toes, ladle out flour, count out nails, measure off yard goods. At last he could stand it no longer, so he put his hero books under his arm and ran away.

O f course he headed west. Not the Far West yet—just an island in the middle of the Tennessee River that was occupied by a band of Cherokee Indians. From all he'd heard, In-dians lived in a free and easy way, which Sam figured would be a nice change.

And it was. Eventually his brothers tracked him down, but they might as well have stayed at home, tending their farm. Sam was lying under a tree read-ing a hero book when they found him. When they told him to get up and get moving, Sam didn't budge. When they argued, Sam waved them away. Please excuse him, he said. He was reading.

Sam stayed with the Cherokees for three years— the best years of his life, he later said. The Cherokee chief, John Jolly, took a fancy to Sam, adopted him as a son, and gave him an Indian name, The Raven.

Sam learned to speak like the Cherokees, to dress like them, to hunt like them, and like them, he had his own medicine animal with special powers over his life. His was the eagle. And each year at corn-ripening time Sam joined in the Green Corn Dance, shucking away the bad in him so that he could, like all Cherokees, start life afresh.

Every once in a while Sam went back to check on civilization, but it didn't seem to improve. So after visiting with his mother and borrowing money so he could buy presents for his Indian friends, he returned to the island. By the end of three years he had piled up a debt of $100. This was a lot of money, and he understood (or he was made to understand) that he had to pay it back and soon. Perhaps by this time he was ready to give civilization another chance, but ready or not, he went back to get a job.

He had no notion, however, of becoming one hundred percent civilized. He kept his hair in a long queue, Indian fashion, down his back. And he decided that when he went to work, he wasn't going to take orders; he was going to give them. Since there were no grown people in Maryville who were interested in taking orders from nineteen-year-old Sam Houston, he opened a school. The price per student, he announced, would be $8 a term.

What a joke! people laughed. Sam Houston teaching school! He must have received his degree from the Indian University. Still, Sam did get enough pupils so that after one term he was able to pay off his debt. And that was enough teaching. What next? He still had big ideas and felt sure that he had a destiny that was waiting for him somewhere but he didn't know what it was or how to find it.

He may have thought about war because one had started in June, 1812, soon after he'd begun to teach.

SURRENDER OF SANTA ANA
AT THE BATTLE OF SAN JACINTO

Texas State Capitol
Courtesy Texas State Highways Magazine

Sam Houston lies wounded.
He is looking at Santa Ana, who is standing
in the center of the group. The
man cupping his ear is Erastus Smith,
a famous scout and important
man in Houston's army.

America was fighting England because England kept butting into America's independence, interfering with American ships at sea, inciting the Western Indians against the United States. It was as if England was trying to get a toehold back on the American continent, which most Americans hoped would one day be theirs from coast to coast.

S till, it was not until March 24, 1813, that Sam actually heard the Hero Call. On that day an army recruiting party marched into Maryville, banners streaming, drums rolling. A sergeant made a patriotic speech to the crowd that gathered; then he tossed a handful of silver dollars on top of a drumhead. Any man who picked up a dollar was then and there a member of the United States Army.

Sam Houston stepped up, picked up a dollar, and dropped it into his pocket. He may have been the only one, for his friends made fun of him for enlisting as a common soldier without even trying for an officer's commission. But at least his mother knew how to give him a proper farewell. Many Americans still held on to ideas left over from the days of knighthood in Europe. A man who was fighting for his country liked to think he was also fighting for a special lady—a sweetheart, a wife, or a mother—one who would send him off with a remembrance and brave words. Mrs. Houston gave Sam a ring with the single word *Honor* inscribed inside. (Sam wore the ring all his life.) And when Sam left, Mrs. Houston made a parting speech. "While the door of my cabin is open to brave men," she said, "it is eternally shut against cowards."

Sam would have to wait over a year, however, before he'd find out if he was brave or not. When at last he did go into battle, it was in Alabama against a tribe of Creek Indians who called themselves the Red Sticks and sided with the English. On March 27, 1814, Sam, an ensign now in charge of a platoon, was with General Andrew Jackson's army as it took its position on one side of a rampart of earth and logs stretched across a peninsula in a horseshoelike bend of the Tallapoosa River. On the other side were the Red Sticks armed with bows, spears, tomahawks, and rifles. Some Red Sticks were hiding in thickets, some concealed in a ravine covered with wood to serve as a fortress, but most were massed and ready for anyone and everyone who dared to scale the rampart. The first American to climb to the top was a Major Montgomery; he was killed on sight. The second was Ensign Sam Houston, leading his platoon and followed by the rest of the army, which did manage to go over the top, though many died on the way.

The battle broke up now into dozens of small battles with Sam in the middle of one, fighting and being fought. Suddenly an arrow shot from a thicket buried itself in Sam's groin. He reached down to pull it out but it was a barbed arrow; it didn't come out. He asked a lieutenant fighting beside him to pull it out, but though the lieutenant tried he couldn't get it out either. The best thing for Sam to do, the lieutenant said, was to find the army doctor.

What? Quit the battle?

Sam pointed his sword at the lieutenant. Try again, he said. So the lieutenant, bracing himself, tugged with all his might and the arrow came out but a lot of Sam came with it. The hole in him was so huge that whether he wanted to or not, Sam had to find

EQUESTRIAN SAM HOUSTON

The San Jacinto Museum
of History Association
Houston, Texas

help to stop the bleeding. A doctor plugged up the hole, and while Sam was lying on the ground, catching his breath, General Jackson stopped to ask about his injury. Sam was not to return to battle, he said.

Actually the battle was going well. The only resistance left was from the little fortress, where the Red Sticks were shooting through tiny window holes they had made. Jackson called for volunteers to take the fortress, but no one wanted to march through the onslaught of bullets pouring from those window holes. No one wanted to shoot at an enemy who couldn't be seen. So Sam, ignoring Jackson's command, got to his feet and ordered his platoon to follow. Perhaps he had read too many hero stories to do anything else. Perhaps this was the first time that Sam Houston had faced anything big enough to challenge his whole mind and his whole body and he had decided it was worth risking his life. But as soon as he came within range of those bullets, he was shot twice in the shoulder and once in the arm. When he collapsed, his platoon would go no farther. In the end Jackson did what perhaps he should have done in the first place. He had the fortress set on fire with flaming arrows.

The Battle of Horseshoe Bend was over and Sam was alive but barely so. Later Sam, who liked to talk about Destiny, may have given Destiny credit for the fact that he came through at all. Yet many times he must have wondered if Destiny was even on the job. The doctors re-dressed Sam's arrow wound and put a splint on his arm, but although they got one bullet out of his shoulder, they couldn't reach the other and decided not to try. That night when they moved the wounded from the field, they left Sam behind among the dead and near-dying. He wouldn't last the night, they said.

But he did last. The next day, along with some other survivors, he was rescued. Placed on a litter made of saplings, he was pulled over sixty miles of rough road to a wilderness fort. The other injured men were taken to a well-equipped station, but Sam seemed so near death no one wanted to cause him more pain. So he was left in the care of two militia officers, neither of whom had any medical experience.

Still Sam did not die. During the next year he was moved from place to place and two more doctors gave him up before a doctor in New Orleans finally got that bullet out of his shoulder. The wound never did completely heal and in early 1815, before he had a chance to fight again, the war was over. The Battle of New Orleans had been fought and won, and Andrew Jackson, the victorious general, was a national hero.

By this time Sam had become a lieutenant and ex-pected to make the army his career. For the sake of the country, he said, he was glad for peace but as an officer he was disappointed. He had hoped to take part in more battles.

Thinking About It

1. Sam Houston admired heroes and loved to read hero stories. What three heroes who have lived since Sam would you make sure he read about if you had the chance? Tell him why he should read about them.

2. Sam Houston didn't always do what he was supposed to do. List some examples. Then, as Sam, justify what you did instead.

3. Sam Houston has been transported to the present. Is there a place for him here? What would he do? Do we still need heroes like Sam Houston?

Another Book About an American Hero
The Great Little Madison by Jean Fritz tells about the fourth President of the United States who, although a quiet and withdrawn man "no bigger than half a piece of soap," made a great contribution to United States history.

Cookies with Mrs. Flowers

*M*rs. Bertha Flowers was the aristocrat of Black Stamps.* She had the grace of control to appear warm in the coldest weather, and on the Arkansas summer days it seemed she had a private breeze which swirled around, cooling her. She was thin without the taut look of wiry people, and her printed voile dresses and flowered hats were as right for her as denim overalls for a farmer. She was our side's answer to the richest white woman in town.

Her skin was a rich black that would have peeled like a plum if snagged, but then no one would have thought of getting close enough to Mrs. Flowers to ruffle her dress, let alone snag her skin. She didn't encourage familiarity. She wore gloves too.

I don't think I ever saw Mrs. Flowers laugh, but she smiled often. A slow widening of her thin black lips to show even, small white teeth, then the slow

*Stamps, Arkansas

effortless closing. When she chose to smile on me, I always wanted to thank her. The action was so graceful and inclusively benign.

She was one of the few gentlewomen I have ever known, and has remained throughout my life the measure of what a human being can be.

Momma* had a strange relationship with her. Most often when she passed on the road in front of the Store, she spoke to Momma in that soft yet carrying voice, "Good day, Mrs. Henderson." Momma responded with "How you, Sister Flowers?"

Mrs. Flowers didn't belong to our church, nor was she Momma's familiar. Why on earth did she insist on calling her Sister Flowers? Shame made me want to hide my face. Mrs. Flowers deserved better than to be called Sister. Then, Momma left out the verb. Why not ask, "How *are* you, *Mrs*. Flowers?" With the unbalanced passion of the young, I hated her for showing her ignorance to Mrs. Flowers. It didn't occur to me for many years that they were as alike as sisters, separated only by formal education.

Although I was upset, neither of the women was in the least shaken by what I thought an unceremonious greeting. Mrs. Flowers would continue her easy gait up the hill to her little bungalow, and Momma kept on shelling peas or doing whatever had brought her to the front porch.

Occasionally, though, Mrs. Flowers would drift off the road and down to the Store and Momma would say to me, "Sister, you go on and play." As I left I would hear the beginning of an intimate conversation. Momma persistently using the wrong verb, or none at all.

"Brother and Sister Wilcox is sho'ly the meanest—" "Is," Momma? "Is"? Oh, please, not "is," Momma,

*Maya Angelou's grandmother

for two or more. But they talked, and from the side of the building where I waited for the ground to open up and swallow me, I heard the soft-voiced Mrs. Flowers and the textured voice of my grandmother merging and melting. They were interrupted from time to time by giggles that must have come from Mrs. Flowers (Momma never giggled in her life). Then she was gone.

She appealed to me because she was like people I had never met personally. Like women in English novels who walked the moors (whatever they were) with their loyal dogs racing at a respectful distance. Like the women who sat in front of roaring fireplaces, drinking tea incessantly from silver trays full of scones and crumpets. Women who walked over the "heath" and read morocco-bound books and had two last names divided by a hyphen. It would be safe to say that she made me proud to be Negro, just by being herself.

She acted just as refined as whitefolks in the movies and books and she was more beautiful, for none of them could have come near that warm color without looking gray by comparison.

*I*t was fortunate that I never saw her in the company of powhitefolks. For since they tend to think of their whiteness as an evenizer, I'm certain that I would have had to hear her spoken to commonly as Bertha, and my image of her would have been shattered like the unmendable Humpty-Dumpty.

One summer afternoon, sweet-milk fresh in my memory, she stopped at the Store to buy provisions. Another Negro woman of her health and age would have been expected to carry the paper sacks home in one hand, but Momma said, "Sister Flowers, I'll send

Bailey up to your house with these things."

She smiled that slow dragging smile, "Thank you, Mrs. Henderson. I'd prefer Marguerite, though." My name was beautiful when she said it. "I've been meaning to talk to her, anyway." They gave each other age-group looks.

Momma said, "Well, that's all right then. Sister, go and change your dress. You going to Sister Flowers's."

The chifforobe was a maze. What on earth did one put on to go to Mrs. Flowers' house? I knew I shouldn't put on a Sunday dress. It might be sacrilegious. Certainly not a house dress, since I was already wearing a fresh one. I chose a school dress, naturally. It was formal without suggesting that going to Mrs. Flowers' house was equivalent to attending church.

I trusted myself back into the Store.

"Now, don't you look nice." I had chosen the right thing, for once.

"Mrs. Henderson, you make most of the children's clothes, don't you?"

"Yes, ma'am. Sure do. Store-bought clothes ain't hardly worth the thread it take to stitch them."

"I'll say you do a lovely job, though, so neat. That dress looks professional."

Momma was enjoying the seldom-received compliments. Since everyone we knew (except Mrs. Flowers, of course) could sew competently, praise was rarely handed out for the commonly practiced craft.

"I try, with the help of the Lord, Sister Flowers, to finish the inside just like I does the outside. Come here, Sister."

I had buttoned up the collar and tied the belt, apronlike, in back. Momma told me to turn around. With one hand she pulled the strings and the belt fell free at both sides of my waist. Then her large hands were at my neck, opening the button loops. I was terrified. What was happening?

"Take it off, Sister." She had her hands on the hem of the dress.

"I don't need to see the inside, Mrs. Henderson, I can tell..." But the dress was over my head and my arms were stuck in the sleeves. Momma said, "That'll do. See here, Sister Flowers, I French-seams around the armholes." Through the cloth film, I saw the shadow approach. "That makes it last longer. Children these days would bust out of sheet-metal clothes. They so rough."

"That is a very good job, Mrs. Henderson. You should be proud. You can put your dress back on, Marguerite."

"No ma'am. Pride is a sin. And 'cording to the Good Book, it goeth before a fall."

"That's right. So the Bible says. It's a good thing to keep in mind."

I wouldn't look at either of them. Momma hadn't thought that taking off my dress in front of Mrs. Flowers would kill me stone dead. If I had refused, she would have thought I was trying to be "woman-

ish" and might have remembered St. Louis. Mrs. Flowers had known that I would be embarrassed and that was even worse. I picked up the groceries and went out to wait in the hot sunshine. It would be fitting if I got a sunstroke and died before they came outside. Just dropped dead on the slanting porch.

There was a little path beside the rocky road, and Mrs. Flowers walked in front swinging her arms and picking her way over the stones.

She said, without turning her head, to me, "I hear you're doing very good schoolwork, Marguerite, but that it's all written. The teachers report that they have trouble getting you to talk in class." We passed the triangular farm on our left and the path widened to allow us to walk together. I hung back in the separate unasked and unanswerable questions.

"Come and walk along with me, Marguerite." I couldn't have refused even if I wanted to. She pronounced my name so nicely. Or more correctly, she spoke each word with such clarity that I was certain a foreigner who didn't understand English could have understood her.

"Now no one is going to make you talk—possibly no one can. But bear in mind, language is man's way of communicating with his fellow man and it is language alone which separates him from the lower animals." That was a totally new idea to me, and I would need time to think about it.

"Your grandmother says you read a lot. Every chance you get. That's good, but not good enough. Words mean more than what is set down on paper. It takes the human voice to infuse them with the shades of deeper meaning."

I memorized the part about the human voice infusing words. It seemed so valid and poetic.

She said she was going to give me some books and

that I not only must read them, I must read them aloud. She suggested that I try to make a sentence sound in as many different ways as possible.

"I'll accept no excuse if you return a book to me that has been badly handled." My imagination boggled at the punishment I would deserve if in fact I did abuse a book of Mrs. Flowers'. Death would be too kind and brief.

*T*he odors in the house surprised me. Somehow I had never connected Mrs. Flowers with food or eating or any other common experience of common people. There must have been an outhouse, too, but my mind never recorded it.

The sweet scent of vanilla had met us as she opened the door.

"I made tea cookies this morning. You see, I had planned to invite you for cookies and lemonade so we could have this little chat. The lemonade is in the icebox."

It followed that Mrs. Flowers would have ice on an ordinary day, when most families in our town bought ice late on Saturdays only a few times during the summer to be used in the wooden ice-cream freezers.

She took the bags from me and disappeared through the kitchen door. I looked around the room that I had never in my wildest fantasies imagined I would see. Browned photographs leered or threatened from the walls and the white, freshly done curtains pushed against themselves and against the wind. I wanted to gobble up the room entire and take it to Bailey, who would help me analyze and enjoy it.

"Have a seat, Marguerite. Over there by the table." She carried a platter covered with a tea towel. Although she warned that she hadn't tried her hand at baking sweets for some time, I was certain that like everything else about her the cookies would be perfect.

They were flat round wafers, slightly browned on the edges and butter-yellow in the center. With the cold lemonade they were sufficient for childhood's lifelong diet. Remembering my manners, I took nice little lady-like bites off the edges. She said she had made them expressly for me and that she had a few in the kitchen that I could take home to my brother. So I jammed one whole cake in my mouth and the rough crumbs scratched the insides of my jaws, and if I hadn't had to swallow, it would have been a dream come true.

As I ate she began the first of what we later called "my lessons in living." She said that I must always be intolerant of ignorance but understanding of illiteracy. That some people, unable to go to school, were more educated and even more intelligent than college professors. She encouraged me to listen carefully to what country people called mother wit. That in those homely sayings was couched the collective wisdom of generations.

When I finished the cookies she brushed off the table and brought a thick, small book from the bookcase. I had read *A Tale of Two Cities* and found it up to my standards as a romantic novel. She opened the first page and I heard poetry for the first time in my life.

"It was the best of times and the worst of times..." Her voice slid in and curved down through and over the words. She was nearly singing. I wanted to look at the pages. Were they the same that I had read? Or were there notes, music, lined on the pages, as in a hymn book? Her sounds began cascading gently. I knew from listening to a thousand preachers that she was nearing the end of her reading, and I hadn't really heard, heard to understand, a single word.

"How do you like that?"

It occurred to me that she expected a response. The sweet vanilla flavor was still on my tongue and her reading was a wonder in my ears. I had to speak.

I said, "Yes, ma'am." It was the least I could do, but it was the most also.

"There's one more thing. Take this book of poems and memorize one for me. Next time you pay me a visit, I want you to recite."

I have tried often to search behind the sophistication of years for the enchantment I so easily found in those gifts. The essence escapes but its aura remains. To be allowed, no, invited, into the private lives of strangers, and to share their joys and fears, was a chance to exchange the Southern bitter wormwood for a cup of mead with Beowulf or a hot cup of tea and milk with Oliver Twist. When I said aloud, "It is a far, far better thing that I do, than I have ever done..." tears of love filled my eyes at my selflessness.

On that first day, I ran down the hill and into the road (few cars ever came along it) and had the good sense to stop running before I reached the Store.

I was liked, and what a difference it made. I was respected not as Mrs. Henderson's grandchild or Bailey's sister but for just being Marguerite Johnson.

Childhood's logic never asks to be proved (all conclusions are absolute). I didn't question why Mrs. Flowers had singled me out for attention, nor did it occur to me that Momma might have asked her to give me a little talking to. All I cared about was that she had made tea cookies for *me* and read to *me* from her favorite book. It was enough to prove that she liked me.

JANINE RICHARDSON

They Made Themselves Heard

In March, 1988, students at Gallaudet University in Washington, D.C., blockaded the campus, boycotted classes, and marched in protest to the nation's Capitol. "DEAF PRESIDENT NOW!" proclaimed the signs and banners of these students who were deaf themselves. They were angry at the choice of yet another hearing person to be the new president at Gallaudet, the only liberal arts college in the world for people with hearing disabilities. Within days, the hearing candidate had withdrawn, and educator I. King Jordan, who is deaf, was announced as the new president at Gallaudet.

The history of deaf people and their education in the United States has often been stormy. Furious disagreement over what is best for these people and what their goals should be raged at the turn of this century. Were they to be "educated" or "rehabilitated"?

Thomas Hopkins Gallaudet established the first permanent school for deaf persons in the United States in 1817. Several years earlier, Gallaudet, who had studied for the ministry at Yale, had met eight-year-old Alice Cogswell, a neighbor of Gallaudet's parents who had lost her hearing at the age of two.

Gallaudet tried to communicate with Alice through writing and the manual alphabet. Encouraged by his interest, Alice's father seized upon Gallaudet as the one to head a school for Alice and others like her. Mr. Cogswell was persuasive, and the initially reluctant Gallaudet was dispatched to Europe in 1815 to learn all that he could about teaching deaf people.

His first stop was in England, where the Braidwood family had become famous for their success in educating persons who were deaf, using oral methods of speech training and lip reading. The Braidwoods greeted Gallaudet with distrust and suspicion. Teaching children from wealthy families was a lucrative business, and they saw no reason to share their secrets. First, they refused to train him. Next, they agreed to have him, but only if he would work with the children from 7:00 A.M. to 8:00 P.M. and stay with them after hours as well.

Refusing this, Gallaudet turned to the National Institution for the Deaf in France. Abbé Sicard, the director of this world famous school, graciously welcomed Gallaudet. The school, which taught students finger spelling and sign language, was open to rich and poor alike. Gallaudet studied in Paris for two months and then returned to the United States. He brought with him one of Abbé Sicard's star pupils and teachers, Laurent Clerc. On the return voyage, Gallaudet studied sign language, and Clerc studied English.

Gallaudet and Clerc opened The American School for the Deaf, originally called The American Asylum, at Hartford, for the Deaf and Dumb, in 1817. The school became the model for other schools for deaf persons then starting up in the United States.

Freed from their isolation, students at these schools came together in an atmosphere of acceptance and hope. They flourished as they learned, prayed, and played together. Teachers who also were deaf acted as role models, daily reminders of what the students could accomplish with education.

Thomas Gallaudet died in 1851, but his son Edward Miner Gallaudet continued his father's work.

In 1857, Edward Gallaudet became director of the new Columbia Institution for Instruction of the Deaf, Dumb and the Blind in Washington, D.C. Seven years later, in 1864, Congress passed a bill authorizing the school to grant college degrees, and President Abraham Lincoln signed the bill into law. The college division of the school was named the National Deaf-Mute College. In 1894, it became Gallaudet College.

Up until 1880, the use of sign language in schools for deaf people was widely accepted. At that time, an international group of educators decided that oral methods were better than manual for educating the deaf. Progress in deaf education was hampered by the bitter fighting between supporters of the two methods.

The manualists' goal was to educate and to teach job skills using sign language. Speech training and lip reading were not emphasized. The oralists wanted students to be able to participate fully in a hearing society. This, they believed, could be accomplished by years of education in speech training and lip reading. By the turn of the century, sign language had been banned from the classroom, along with teachers who also were deaf. Children used sign in secret, but if they were caught, they often had their hands tied or were otherwise punished.

Today, sign is respected as a legitimate language and is used widely in the education of students who are deaf. At Gallaudet, students can study for a liberal arts degree entirely in sign. Teachers who have hearing disabilities also have made a comeback and once again serve as role models for the students they teach.

PULLING IT ALL TOGETHER

1. "Cookies with Mrs. Flowers" and "They Made Themselves Heard" are about very different subjects. What idea links the two selections? Which selection has more meaning for you personally? Explain.

2. Sometimes people have experiences, like Marguerite's in "Cookies with Mrs. Flowers," which they remember as a special time or as a turning point in their lives. Tell about the experiences that some of the other characters in this book would remember.

3. Now it's your turn. It's fifty years in the future. You're going to write about your life. What challenges did you meet? Was there someone who helped you reach your goals? Did you rise to the occasion? Did you take on a cause? What details would you include to write a good book?

BOOKS TO ENJOY

MANIAC MAGEE
by Jerry Spinelli
Harper, 1991
They say lots of things about Maniac Magee—that he was born in a dump, had an eight-inch cockroach, scared ghosts, and was the fastest runner alive. But he was also just a kid trying to find a home.

CHILD OF THE OWL
by Laurence Yep
Harper, 1977
Casey's dad has a hard time providing a steady income, so she is sent to live in Chinatown. Her world changes when her grandmother shares her own past, along with a special jade charm.

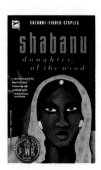

SHABANU, DAUGHTER OF THE WIND
by Suzanne Fisher Staples
Knopf, 1989
Is your world like hers? Shabanu grows up in the Pakistani desert, where people and animals live and perish. Her world has camel bells, gold bangles, sandstorms, campfires, and an exotic wedding.

VOYAGE OF THE FROG
by Gary Paulsen
Franklin Watts, 1989
David Alspeth sets out alone to scatter his uncle's ashes at sea in the Pacific when a storm overtakes his sailboat, the *Frog.*

PEOPLE WHO MAKE A DIFFERENCE
by Brent Ashabranner
Dutton, 1989
A country doctor, a karate teacher, a friend of sea turtles, and a Dallas police officer are among the enterprising people who make the world a better place.

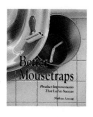

BETTER MOUSETRAPS: PRODUCT IMPROVEMENTS THAT LED TO SUCCESS
by Nathan Aaseng
Lerner, 1990
Eight innovators gained fame by improving everyday products, from fancy cars to bread. The world can always use a better mousetrap, you know.

REDWALL
by Brian Jacques
Philomel, 1986
Matthias the monastery mouse seems a most unlikely hero. You'll be drawn into his fantastic quests and adventures as he defends Redwall Abbey against a rat scourge.

LITERARY TERMS

AUTOBIOGRAPHY AND BIOGRAPHY While an autobiography is the story of a real person's life written by that person, a biography is the story of a real person's life written by another person. "What? Quit the Battle?" and "Who Is This Nellie Bly?" are selections from biographies, as is "Gordon Parks: Focus on America."

CHARACTER A character is a person or an animal in a play or story. The main character is the one most important to the story. Virtue and Maniac Magee are main characters who are "larger than life." Both perform unbelievable feats that amaze other characters. As readers, we learn about Maniac Magee and Virtue through their own actions and through the reactions of others to them.

IMAGERY Imagery is used to help readers experience the way things look, sound, smell, taste, or feel. In "Billie Wind Listens to Her Land," there are many descriptions that are lively and imaginative. For example, the air outside as Billie Wind listens to Charlie Wind is "white and hot." Later, at Lost Dog Slough, a burning tree falling into the water "hissed like a snake."

NARRATOR The author's choice of narrator determines how the actions and characters of a story will be presented. An all-knowing outsider who can enter the minds of the characters and give information about every character in the story is said to be an omniscient narrator. "Maniac Magee and Cobble's Knot" is told from the omniscient point of view.

NOVEL A novel is a long work of fiction that includes the story elements of character, setting, plot, and theme. "Maniac Magee and Cobble's Knot" and "Billie Wind Listens to Her Land" are from novels.

ONOMATOPOEIA Onomatopoeia is a term used for words that sound like their meanings. It is a device used to reinforce meaning and add drama to a story. Words like *screeched, buzzing,* and *beep* in "Maniac Magee and Cobble's Knot" are examples of onomatopoeia, as are *whoop* and *swishes* in "Basketball Bragging."

SIMILE A simile is a comparison of two unlike things signaled by the word *like* or the word *as*. Notice the comparison of stars to schools of fish in the following example from the story about the star fisher: ". . . the stars wriggled and shimmered like schools of fish."

STYLE Style of writing is determined by the author's choice and arrangement of words, and it reflects the author's ideas and purpose. One part of an author's style is the way the story seems to move—its pace. For example, the pace of "Billie Wind Listens to Her Land" is slow—the description of setting is more important than the movement of the plot.

GLOSSARY

Vocabulary from your selections

be nign (bi nīn′), *adj.* **1** kindly in feeling; benevolent; gracious: *a benign old woman.* **2** showing a kindly feeling; gentle: *a benign countenance.* **3** favorable.

borne (bôrn, bōrn), *v.* a past participle of **bear:** *I have borne it as long as I can.*

chignon

cal dron (kôl′drən), *n.* a large kettle or boiler. Also, **cauldron.**

chap e ron or **chap e rone** (shap′ə rōn′), *n., v.,* **-roned, -ron ing.** —*n.* **1** an older person who is present at a party or other social activity of young people to see that good taste is observed. **2** a person, especially a married or an older woman, who accompanies a young unmarried woman in public for the sake of propriety. —*v.t.* act as a chaperon to; escort.

chi gnon (shē′nyon; *French* shē nyôn′), *n.* a large knot or roll of hair worn at the back of the head.

cir cu la tion (sėr′kyə lā′shən), *n.* **1** a going around; circulating: *Open windows increase the circulation of air in a room.* **2** flow of the blood from the heart through the arteries and veins back to the heart. **3** a sending around of books, papers, news, etc., from person to person or from place to place. **4** the number of copies of a book, newspaper, magazine, etc., that are sent out during a certain time.

cloak (klōk), *n.* **1** a loose outer garment with or without sleeves; mantle. **2** anything that covers or conceals; outward show; mask. —*v.t.* **1** cover with a cloak. **2** cover up; conceal; hide.

com mis sion (kə mish′ən), *n.* **1** a written order giving certain powers, privileges, and duties. **2** a written order giving rank and authority as an officer in the armed forces. **3** rank and authority given by such an order. —*v.t.* **1** give (a person) the power, right, or duty (to do something); give authority to; license; authorize; empower. **2** give a commission to.

com mu nal (kə myü′nl, kom′yə nəl), *adj.* **1** of a community; public. **2** owned jointly by all; used or participated in by all members of a group or community. **3** of a commune.

con tor tion (kən tôr′shən), *n.* **1** a twisting or bending out of shape; distorting. **2** a contorted condition; distorted form or shape.

con tro ver sial (kon′trə vėr′shəl), *adj.* **1** of or having to do with controversy. **2** open to controversy; debatable; disputed: *a controversial question.* **3** fond of controversy; argumentative. —**con′tro ver′sial ly,** *adv.*

con tro ver sy (kon′trə vėr′sē), *n., pl.* **-sies.** **1** an arguing a question about which differences of opinion exist. **2** quarrel; wrangle.

des ti ny (des′tə nē), *n., pl.* **-nies. 1** what becomes of a person or thing in the end; one's lot or fortune. **2** what will happen in spite of all later efforts to change or prevent it.

dug out (dug′out′), *n.* **1** a rough shelter or cave dug into the side of a hill, trench, etc., and often reinforced with logs, used for protection against bullets and bombs. **2** a small shelter at the side of a baseball field, used by players who are not at bat or not in the game. **3** a crude boat made by hollowing out a large log.

e on (ē′ən, ē′on), *n.* a very long period of time; many thousands of years.

ex hil a rate (eg zil′ə rāt′), *v.t.*, **-rat ed, -rat ing.** make merry or lively; put into high spirits; cheer.

fan cy (fan′sē), *v.*, **-cied, -cy ing,** *n., pl.* **-cies,** *adj.*, **-ci er, -ci est.** —*v.t.* **1** picture to oneself; imagine; conceive: *Can you fancy yourself on the moon?* **2** be fond of; like: *I fancy the idea of having a picnic.* —*n.* **1** power to imagine; imagination; fantasy: *Dragons and giants are creatures of fancy.* **2** something imagined. **3** something supposed; idea; notion: *I had a sudden fancy to go swimming.* **4** a liking; fondness: *They took a great fancy to each other.* —*adj.* made or arranged especially to please; valued for beauty rather than use; decorated.

fel low ship (fel′ō ship), *n.* **1** condition or quality of being a fellow; companionship; friendship. **2** position or money given by a university or college to a graduate student to enable him or her to continue studying.

frag ile (fraj′əl), *adj.* easily broken, damaged, or destroyed; delicate; frail. —**frag′ile ly,** *adv.*

fric as see (frik′ə sē′), *n., v.*, **-seed, -see ing.** —*n.* chicken or other meat cut up, stewed, and served in a sauce made with its own gravy. —*v.t.* prepare (meat) in this way.

hal lowed (hal′ōd; *in church use, often* hal′ō id), *adj.* **1** made holy; sacred; consecrated: *A churchyard is hallowed ground.* **2** honored or observed as holy.

hu mus (hyü′məs), *n.* a dark-brown or black part of soil formed from decayed leaves and other vegetable matter, containing valuable plant foods.

in dict ment (in dīt′mənt), *n.* **1** a formal written accusation, especially one presented by a grand jury. **2** accusation.

in fuse (in fyüz′), *v.t.*, **-fused, -fus ing. 1** introduce as by pouring; put in; instill: *The captain infused his own courage into his soldiers.* **2** inspire: *The soldiers were infused with his courage.*

in jus tice (in jus′tis), *n.* **1** lack of justice; being unjust. **2** an unjust act.

jaun ty (jôn′tē, jän′tē), *adj.*, **-ti er, -ti est. 1** easy and lively; sprightly; carefree: *The happy children walked with jaunty steps.* **2** smart; stylish: *She wore a jaunty little hat.*

a hat	oi oil
ā age	ou out
ä far	u cup
e let	u̇ put
ē equal	ü rule
ėr term	
i it	ch child
ī ice	ng long
o hot	sh she
ō open	th thin
ô order	ᴛʜ then
	zh measure

ə = { a in about
e in taken
i in pencil
o in lemon
u in circus }

< = derived from

dugout (def. 3)

kingfisher

king fish er (king′fish′ər), *n.* any of numerous crested, bright-colored birds with large heads and strong beaks. Kingfishers eat fish and insects, and are found in most parts of the world.

lithe (līᴛH), *adj.* bending easily; supple: *lithe of body, a lithe willow.* —**lithe′ly**, *adv.* —**lithe′ness**, *n.*

lynch (linch), *v.t.* put (an accused person) to death, usually by hanging, without a lawful trial.

man u al (man′yü əl), *adj.* of or having to do with the hands; done with the hands: *manual labor.*

manual alphabet, finger alphabet.

me thod i cal (mə thod′ə kəl), *adj.* **1** done according to a method; systematic; orderly. **2** acting with method or order: *a methodical person.* —**me-thod′i cal ly**, *adv.*

mi li tia (mə lish′ə), *n.* a military force consisting especially of citizens trained for war, emergency duty, or the national defense.

mod est (mod′ist), *adj.* **1** having or showing a moderate estimate of one's merits, importance, achievements, etc.; not vain; humble: *The prize-winning scientist remained a modest man.* **2** held back by a sense of what is fit and proper; not bold or forward.

mug gy (mug′ē), *adj.,* **-gi er, -gi est.** warm and humid; damp and close: *muggy weather.*

non de script (non′də skript), *adj.* not easily classified; not of any one particular kind: *We drove past a block of nondescript houses.* —*n.* a nondescript person or thing.

om i nous (om′ə nəs), *adj.* unfavorable; threatening: *ominous clouds.* —**om′i nous ly**, *adv.*

o ral (ôr′əl, ōr′əl), *adj.* **1** using speech; spoken: *an oral command.* **2** of the mouth: *oral hygiene.*

per plex (pər pleks′), *v.t.* **1** trouble with doubt; puzzle; bewilder. **2** make difficult to understand or settle; confuse.

phe nom e non (fə nom′ə non), *n., pl.* **-na** (or **-nons** for 4). **1** fact, event, or circumstance that can be observed: *Lightning is an electrical phenomenon.* **2** any sign, symptom, or manifestation: *Fever and inflammation are phenomena of disease.* **3** any exceptional fact or occurrence: *historical phenomena.* **4** an extraordinary or remarkable person or thing.

price less (prīs′lis), *adj.* **1** beyond price; extremely valuable. **2** INFORMAL. very amusing, absurd, etc.; delightful.

pro found (prə found′), *adj.* **1** very deep: *a profound sigh, a profound sleep.* **2** deeply felt; very great: *profound despair, profound sympathy.* **3** going far deeper than what is easily understood; having or showing great knowledge or understanding: *a profound book, a profound thought.*

pro nounce ment (prə nouns′mənt), *n.* **1** a formal or authoritative statement; declaration. **2** opinion or decision.

pro voc a tive (prə vok′ə tiv), *adj.* **1** irritating; vexing. **2** tending or serving to call forth action, thought, laughter, anger, etc.: *a provocative remark.* —*n.* something that rouses or irritates.

queue (kyü), *n.* **1** braid of hair hanging down from the back of the head. **2** a line of people, automobiles, etc.: *There was a long queue in front of the theater.*

rac ism (rā′siz′əm), *n.* **1** belief that a particular race, especially one's own, is superior to other races. **2** discrimination or prejudice against a race or races based on this belief.

ram part (ram′pärt), *n.* **1** a wide bank of earth, often with a wall on top as a fortification, built around a fort to help defend it. **2** anything that defends; defense; protection.

re fined (ri find′), *adj.* **1** freed from impurities; made pure: *refined sugar.* **2** free from vulgarity; cultivated; well-bred: *refined tastes, refined manners.* **3** minutely precise; fine; subtle.

re mem brance (ri mem′brəns), *n.* **1** power to remember; act of remembering; memory. **2** condition of being remembered. **3** any thing or action that makes one remember a person; keepsake; souvenir.

rep ri mand (rep′rə mand), *n.* a severe or formal reproof. —*v.t.* reprove severely or formally.

sac ri le gious (sak′rə lij′əs, sak′rə lē′jəs), *adj.* injurious or insulting to sacred persons or things.

shan ty (shan′tē), *n., pl.* **-ties.** a roughly built hut or cabin.

shuck (shuk), *n.* **1** husk, pod, or shell, especially the outer covering or strippings of corn, chestnuts, hickory nuts, etc. **2** shell of an oyster or clam. —*v.t.* **1** remove the husk, pod, or shell from: *shuck corn.* **2** take off; remove.

sink hole (singk′hōl′), *n.* **1** hole that drains surface water. **2** hole where water collects.

smirk (smėrk), *v.i.* smile in an affected, silly, or self-satisfied way; simper. —*n.* an affected, silly, or self-satisfied smile.

so phis ti ca tion (sə fis′tə kā′shən), *n.* **1** a lessening or loss of naturalness, simplicity, or frankness; worldly experience or ideas; artificial ways.

tes ta ment (tes′tə mənt), *n.* **1** written instructions telling what to do with a person's property after the person dies; will. **2** expression; manifestation. **3** statement of beliefs or principles.

un err ing (un ėr′ing, un er′ing), *adj.* making no mistakes; exactly right: *unerring aim.*

weath er ing (weꜰH′ər ing), *n.* the destructive or discoloring action of air, water, frost, etc., especially on rocks.

a	hat	oi	oil
ā	age	ou	out
ä	far	u	cup
e	let	u̇	put
ē	equal	ü	rule
ėr	term		
i	it	ch	child
ī	ice	ng	long
o	hot	sh	she
ō	open	th	thin
ô	order	ꜰH	then
		zh	measure

ə = { a in about
e in taken
i in pencil
o in lemon
u in circus }

< = derived from

weathering

ACKNOWLEDGMENTS

Text

Page 6: "Maniac Magee and Cobble's Knot" from *Maniac Magee* by Jerry Spinelli. Copyright © 1990 by Jerry Spinelli. By permission of Little, Brown and Company.

Page 16: "Where Maniac Came From," by Jerry Spinelli. Copyright © 1991 by Jerry Spinelli.

Page 20: "basketball" from *Spin a Soft Black Song* by Nikki Giovanni. Copyright © 1971, 1985 by Nikki Giovanni. Reprinted by permission of Farrar, Straus and Giroux, Inc.

Page 21: "Basketball Bragging" reprinted with permission of Margaret K. McElderry Books, an imprint of Macmillan Publishing Company, from *Ghastlies, Goops & Pincushions* by X. J. Kennedy.

Page 56: "Virtue Goes to Town," pp. 136–142 text and art from *The Rainbow People* by Laurence Yep. Illustrated by David Wiesner. Text copyright © 1989 by Laurence Yep. Illustrations copyright © 1989 by David Wiesner. Reprinted by permission of HarperCollins Publishers.

Page 64: "Explorers in a Different Country" from *The Star Fisher* by Laurence Yep. Copyright © 1991 by Laurence Yep. Published by Morrow Junior Books. Reprinted by permission of William Morrow and Company, Inc./Publishers, New York.

Page 78: "Starting at a Penny a Word," by Laurence Yep. Copyright © 1991 by Laurence Yep.

Page 82: "Gordon Parks: Focus on America" from *Gordon Parks* by Skip Berry. Copyright © 1991 by Chelsea House Publishers, a division of Main Line Book Co. All rights reserved. Reprinted by permission.

Page 94: "Who Is This Nellie Bly?" reprinted with permission of Dillon Press, an imprint of Macmillan Publishing Company from *Making Headlines: A Biography of Nellie Bly* by Kathy Lynn Emerson. Copyright © 1991 by Dillon Press.

Page 108: "What? Quit the Battle?" from *Make Way for Sam Houston* by Jean Fritz, text copyright © 1986 by Jean Fritz. Reprinted by permission of G. P. Putnam's Sons.

Page 120: "Cookies with Mrs. Flowers," pages 90–98 from *I Know Why the Caged Bird Sings* by Maya Angelou. Copyright © 1969 by Maya Angelou. Reprinted by permission of Random House, Inc.

Page 130: "They Made Themselves Heard" by Janine Richardson. Originally titled "Teaching Students with Hearing Disabilities" in *Cobblestone's* June, 1989 issue: *People with Disabilities*, © 1989, Cobblestone Publishing, Inc., Peterborough, NH 03458. Reprinted by permission of the publisher.

Artists

Steve Ewert, Cover, 3, 4, 135
Naomi Spellman, Cover, 3, 4, 16, 78, 135
Reneé Flower, Cover, 1, 3, 4, 135, 136, 138, 140
Fran O'Neil, 6–15, 17–19
Jeff Jackson, 20–21
Heather Cooper, 22–55
David Wiesner, 56
Terry Widener, 63
Greg Spalenka, 65, 76, 81
Mary Lempa/Flock Illustrations, 93, 107, 119
Tony Wade, 120, 125

Photographs

Page 16: Courtesy of Jerry Spinelli
Page 78: Courtesy of Laurence Yep
Page 82: Toni Parks-Parsons
Page 86: Standard Oil N J Cole Photographic Archives, University of Louisville
Page 91: Gordon Parks
Page 94: Brown Brothers
Pages 98–99: Carnegie Library of Pittsburgh
Page 104: Library of Congress
Page 131: Francois Robert
Page 133: Jeff Beatty

Glossary

The contents of the Glossary entries in this book have been adapted from *Advanced Dictionary*. Copyright © 1988 Scott, Foresman and Company.

Page 140: The Granger Collection, New York
Page 141: David Austen/Stock Boston
Page 142: Dr. M. P. Kahl/Photo Researchers, Inc.
Page 143: Alan Carey/Stock Boston

Unless otherwise acknowledged, all photographs are the property of ScottForesman.

Illustrations owned and copyrighted by the illustrator.